Faith, Family, and Fairways

By

Bill Cordivari

ISBN 978-1-4958-1453-2

Cover design by Jaclyn McGill

Front cover photography by Jim Britt, M.D.
Hole #8 at Sunrise, Mountain Air Country Club,
Burnsville, North Carolina

Back cover photography by Bruce Cordivari

Editor-in-Chief was Adrienne Basara

Published August 2017

INFINITY PUBLISHING
1094 New DeHaven Street, Suite 100
West Conshohocken, PA 19428-2713
Toll-free (877) BUY BOOK
Local Phone (610) 941-9999
Fax (610) 941-9959
Info@buybooksontheweb.com
www.buybooksontheweb.com

To Mom and Dad

CONTENTS

INTRODUCTION

"Follow the joy." That is the advice my good friend and mentor, Dr. Stephen Payne, suggested to me as I was pondering my priorities across several work and writing options. And it then became the guiding light in writing and finishing *Faith, Family, and Fairways*. The author is always fighting that self-editor who whispers many unhelpful critical thoughts such as, *You stink … that's no good … who would want to read this?* But as you hold this book in your hands and read this page, you bear witness to the fact that the self-editor was defeated.

This is a book mainly about joy, but also the close relative of joy which is gratitude. The things of life which give me the greatest joy and for which I am eternally grateful all revolve around my inspiring faith, my large loving family, and the pursuit of golf, a wonderful game that has long held a grip on me.

On the following pages, I will share with you how these all come together. Most of my friends are also people of faith, as are most of my family. Most of my extensive golfing associates are my friends or family, hence these three facets of my life are tightly interwoven. And I have found that many life lessons revealed in my faith walk have parallels in the world of golf and vice versa. Yes, they do! And why would they not, since a loving God and Creator of all is at the center of history and all created things.

My wish and intent is that you find the stories in this short book inspirational, aspirational, and provocative. May this reading provoke a renewed or reenergized pursuit of your own faith walk. I hope that it helps you see what a blessing our families and loved ones are and that you experience the joy in this realm, or if there is family strife, that you be the one to create the joy. I hope that it motivates you to play more golf or take up the game and see the majesty of creation all around you and experience the game with a heart full of gratitude as you do.

Thank you, dear reader, for sharing your valuable time with *Faith, Family, and Fairways*. And may I share with you the verses below, which are my daily personal call to joy and gratitude:

> *"Rejoice in the Lord always. I will say it again, Rejoice! Let your gentleness be evident to all. The Lord is near. Do not be anxious about anything but in everything by prayer and petition, with thanksgiving, present your requests to God."*
> - Philippians 4:4–6

Chapter 1

ABBA

"As the tree is bent so it grows."
      - Sister Mary Joseph,
        Annunciation Elementary School

" **B**ill, you need to have a talk with him today."

"Okay, I will."

I was in the adjoining room when I overheard the conversation between my mother and father. *Uh-oh, not good*, I thought to myself. The first voice was my mother handing down the directive. The second voice was that of my father, not one to waste words. I knew that I had been busted and was in trouble now.

The setting was early in my freshman year at Villanova and the situation was that I had stopped going to church on Sundays. My thinking was along the lines of, *Come on, I was in college now and part of the enlightened class. I did not need church, God, or any of this other nonsense anymore.*

My father pulled me aside and said, "Let's go out back — we need to have a talk."

Not good. We never had talks with my dad unless we had really screwed up. To my shock and surprise, he started right in on me with no intro or setup. In today's parlance, he was in my face.

"What's up with you? Are you some kind of wise ass?"

You need to know my father never used swear words so I knew he was making a point that this was serious.

"What do you mean saying you aren't going to church anymore?"

I went on about how church was boring, I got nothing out of it, I was in college making my own decisions now.

"Well, let me tell you something, Junior. As long as you are living in this house, you are going to church. It is important to have God and church in your life. If you don't like the church we go to, there are a hundred different churches around here. Pick one. But you are going to church on Sundays."

I could feel my cheeks getting red. Truth be told I was a rebellious teenager, but my father was also my idol. I was a combination of ticked off, embarrassed, and confused. Also resigned. I was not about to invest anytime looking for a new church because I did not care enough.

"Fine," I grumbled, "I will just keep going to our church."

Years later—actually decades later—my faith caught fire. But I could always look back and connect the dots to that conversation with my father, which provided a small spark, a pilot light that just kept burning until the right moment. It not only affected me but taught me how I might impact others. It taught me for the first time that we never know the impact we have on others by our example or profession of belief. We may not get an immediate noticeable response, but we just might be leaving an imprint. I owe my father more than I can enumerate. He was my teacher and role model in many areas, but most importantly in matters of faith and family. Later on, the fairway part would work its way in.

***

I have given you a taste of my faith journey. Let me give you a quick overview of my family in the ensuing pages.

Mom and Dad married in 1948. I was born in 1949 and over the next twelve years in succession were born Richard, Robert, Adrienne, Bruce, and Mark. Yep, five boys and little sister. One big happy family. And I mean that. No qualifiers.

With this quick backdrop, I want to share a special story from a day golfing with Rob, Rich, and Dad. The story centers on the "senior tees." For those who don't know, a golf course has four to five different sets of tees, ranging from Championship, which are the longest, to the Seniors, which are the shortest. This usually knocks 50–100 yards off the length of the hole to reflect that as we age, we cannot drive the ball as far. And this is an attempt to even out competitiveness. But we still should be able to chip, pitch, putt, and play out of the sand. In other words, the short or finesse shots should still be competitive and less dependent upon age and strength.

But there is some psychology at work here as well. As one transitions to the senior tees, one must acknowledge that the body and physical prowess is on the decline and not what it used to be. It can be difficult to accept that one is "moving to the senior tees." Thus was the case in late spring 2014 when we were all together at an annual charity golf outing held in Maryland. Things were shaping up to be a great day. It was sunny and beautiful with Rich, Rob, Dad, and I playing as a team.

We were listening to the announcer giving the instructions, in the midst of a mob scene of hundreds of golfers standing around. The announcer was informing everyone of the local rules for the day. When he got to the last rule, he was talking about which tees people are to play from, and he says: "Seniors will play from the forward green tees." Somebody yells out, "What is your definition of a senior?" And he replies: "Anyone over sixty." Wow! A muffled laugh percolates through the crowd. Many golf courses have senior designated as age sixty-five, others as age sixty-two—but sixty! Gulp.

So the family foursome had one of those collective, out-of-body experiences, as the three brothers all over sixty years old stared at one another. If there was a thought bubble, it would read, *I have not reached geezer age yet, and I am not playing from the senior tees!* Then we look at my father, his shoulders slumped with a quizzical look on his face. He says, "Boy, do I feel old today."

We all had a good laugh. But Rich, Rob, and I resolutely said: "No, we are not playing from the senior tees. We will play back from the competitive middle tees."

And my dad, who still loves to compete and win, says, "No. Come on guys, play from the green tees! We need the advantage if we have any chance of winning."

And we said, "No, Dad, we're playing from the middle tees."

With mild disappointment, he replies, "Okay."

So off we go. It was a fun family day, but from a golf standpoint the three brothers played rather mediocre. We only scored two points that day (I won't belabor the point scoring system with you), thanks to the play of my father who at age ninety sank two very long putts of 30 and 60 feet. After he made the 60-foot putt, he would not let us leave the green until he paced it off and measured it. Dad smirked, "Only 60 feet. Not my personal record of 65 feet!"

***

We went on to have a great dinner, won some raffle prizes, had a few beers, and were flat out exhausted around 8:00 PM when it was time to get going. Thank goodness my brother Rich had volunteered to be the designated driver! Heading back to the Philadelphia area from Maryland, a hot night with the cool of the air conditioning blowing on our faces and nearly everyone falling asleep except for our driver, we all settled into our rhythm. There was a peaceful silence. In the midst of this, we heard this small voice coming from the back seat. It was my father speaking, "One more time, guys, let me ask: why wouldn't you play from the green tees?"

As the eldest son, speaking for the trio, I responded: "Dad … um…. Okay … we are just not ready to admit we are old yet."

He said, "Okay, but we could have scored so many points had you all played from the senior tees!"

I replied, "Okay, what do you think, guys? Dad, we commit to you that next year, we WILL play from the senior tees."

***

From the Bible, I know that I have an Abba (literal, "Daddy") in heaven. Abba is an all-loving and caring father. How blessed I am to have a loving creator in eternity and a loving father in this life. I never take it for granted when I see all the brokenness around me in this world. Mom and Dad and Abba are three key people who fuel my attitude of joy and gratitude.

God and Golf Moment

Find a Great Instructor

Whether it is growing in the faith or growing in golf proficiency, there are great benefits to having mentors, role models, and instructors to impart knowledge and show you how it is done correctly. I have been blessed by great pastors of the faith and great golf professionals of the game.

It is a much tougher and longer journey when we attempt to go about any challenging endeavor alone.

It is not wise to reinvent the wheel. Why waste precious time? Find a trailblazer and ask them to help show you the way.

With golf, I believe finding a great golf professional and instructor who you can connect with and understands you and the game is the only way to become proficient. I learned this the hard way after too many years of trying to teach myself. All I ended up doing was compounding bad habits and incorrect technique.

If you want to accelerate your faith walk—find great mentors, teachers and trailblazers. Learn from them and hang onto them!

And I am grateful to my parents for being my family's best instructors in faith and life.

Chapter 2

ANNA ASSUNTA

"I am the Lord's servant," Mary answered,
"May it be as you have said."

- Luke 1:38

M y mother was her children's greatest
cheerleader. How many people can make
that claim? Probably more than I think, but sadly
not enough. One of my mother's lasting imprints
on my life was her belief that I could be successful,
and through association I picked up that belief.
It was a perfect complement with my father who
had very high standards of expectations for our
personal behaviors and our grade achievements.
Dad set the bar high and Mom said, "You can
do it." This was a great parenting combination.
But my parents' greatest gift was unconditional
boundless love. My parents both emanated the
message that the most important things in their
lives were their children and each other. And
family was first and, by definition, that included
the large extended Italian family of aunts, uncles,
cousins, nieces, nephews, and grandparents.

Besides setting down high standards and expectations, my mom and dad were a great complement to each other and their children in other ways as well. Dad was usually the greatest optimist in the world and my mother could be the biggest pessimist. Maybe God brought them together to protect each other from their polar world views? If we were watching television and someone was being interviewed, my mom might say, "Oh, he is such a liar!" My dad would say, "Oh, I think he is a nice guy," and mom would come back with, "He is such a *stunad* (Italian slang for stupid), and dad would say, "He has a tough job." And back and forth like this it would go.

Again I think of what an awesome dynamic duo they were raising their children, contributing a wonderful blend of encouragement and high standards. A vignette etched in my memory that captures this is a scene from grade school (we used to call it grade school back then before the gradations of elementary, middle, junior, senior, etc.): of coming home with a 98 test score from a math exam. And since like most people I found math quite challenging, I could not wait to get home and share the good news with my parents. My mother's reaction was a big hug, beaming smile, and something along the lines of "Billy, you are so smart!" She then taped my test to the refrigerator. When my dad got home after the obligatory hug, kiss, and hello, I said, "Dad, look, I got a 98 in math today!" And after a pause and with a smile, he said, "Ninety-eight? So close. Why couldn't you get 100?"

As a kid, yes my reaction was probably a tad of disappointment. I think I expected a high five, a "Way to go!" and "You are so smart!" but that was not my dad's way. Discussion of my achievement had ended and Dad moved on to tend to the other events of the day with his wife and other five children.

All of this parental training paid dividends when I was on my own and entered the corporate world. Those who did best in my observation were individuals with high standards and secure egos who did not need constant reinforcement or others constantly telling them how great they were. Mom and Dad's combination training served me and my siblings well.

But back to Mom: the thing that stands out most about my mom was that she was "all in" before "all in" was even part of the lexicon. She was "all in" for her husband and children. It was often as though she did not have a life and that she just lived to serve her family and give unsolicited advice on how you should behave: "Are you going to Aunt Philomena's eighty-fifth birthday party? You should go." "What do you mean you can't go?" "That is a lame excuse." "You are such an ungrateful brat!" ("Brat" was one of my mom's favorite words.) She often called us a brat if we one-upped her in a debate or did not see things her way. But it was an endearing word. To be called a brat by my mom meant that she really loved you and cared about you but thought you were making the wrong decision.

My mom was not an over-controlling mom but she was protective. And she had an opinion on everything. Some of her opinions seemed crazy at the time. Others might make you shake your head or laugh, but they were all well-intentioned and with one single goal: doing what was best for her family and trying to ensure that they all got all that was due them. And looking back, she was probably right with her opinions 90 percent of the time. That is a pretty good percentage in any endeavor.

My parents placed high priority on our education, homework, and grades. They never said that the motivation was to get a great job or make a lot of money. I never heard any of that talk. It was more that we were being taught that we live in a world of right versus wrong, good versus bad, the norm versus the abnormal. If you were going to school, then the purpose of school and the right, good, normal expectation was to get an education and you measured that by grades. Therefore, it was expected that you should get the highest grades you could. This played out in a number of memorable ways.

I grew up through eighth grade in Havertown outside of Philadelphia. When I was about to enter high school, we moved to Rosemont and into the "Big House," which is what we called it — though it is not big by today's standards. Moving to a new neighborhood and school, however, was a key juncture point moment. I had a significant choice to make in terms of which high school I would attend. I had the choice of attending Monsignor Bonner, where all my Havertown friends would be going, or I could go to Cardinal O'Hara, which was a brand-new school not yet open, where Catholic students from Rosemont and environs would be attending. I had no friends in Rosemont. I knew no one. I wanted to go to Bonner, the safe comfortable decision. My parents pushed for O'Hara. In so many words that a parent would communicate to an adolescent, I can now look back and see that they were saying: *Don't always go with the comfortable decision. Don't look back. Don't be afraid of the new. Make a fresh start.*

The decision to go to Cardinal O'Hara was the right decision on multiple planes in terms of life lessons. But my parents were mainly being practical, which was one of their great strengths. The practical implication here was: you are moving to a new neighborhood, you will meet new friends, you will want to go to school with them. They were right on all counts. It was a great juncture point decision. And on top of that, several of my good friends from Havertown went to Villanova, so when I got to college I got to reconnect with them.

Cardinal O'Hara was a large school with a student body of over 4,000 students at the time. "Massive" would be an accurate description. The school was divided into two wings, with boys on one side and girls on the other. There was a sliding gate that was open or closed at various times. On one side, thousands of female classmates were — in the mind of an adolescent male — so close yet so far. One of the older priests — he was probably forty at the time! — said, "Gentlemen, if you are even thinking about them, you are violating the Commandment, "Thou shalt not commit adultery." We were also regularly told to control our "concupiscence." This word is etched in my vocabulary archives from high school and I cannot find anyone today who knows the meaning. I started thinking I made the whole thing up. But I looked it up in the dictionary and I my memory was correct.

Con-cu-pis-cense — Noun. From the Greek, to long for, yearn or have; From the Latin, to covet ardently; In plain English, strong sexual desire; lust.

There you have it. Such were the daily admonitions at Cardinal O'Hara Catholic High School!

The girls had to wear uniforms that were constructed scientifically to hide any curves or suggestions of budding womanhood, and were to be hemmed just at the knee. If it was above the knee, the nuns cut the hem so it would cover the knees and the poor young lady had to walk around that way all day as though bearing a Scarlet Letter of shame.

Several similar noteworthy episodes shaped my high school experience. Would I do it all over again? Absolutely! My four years at Cardinal O'Hara were full of rich personalities of priests, nuns, disciplinarians, classmates, and high standards. I learned high standards as it pertained to education, ethics, and adherence to the moral code laid down by our faith. Were some things over the top? Yes—looking back, I think so. But in all, I view my experiences in Catholic high school as a net positive. I literally had the fear of God instilled into me and that is not necessarily a bad thing. Later in my faith journey I would learn to accept and embrace the love of God, but I think fear and love of the Almighty is a good healthy spiritual balance.

High school was a very difficult time of transition for me, compounded by the move across town and having to make new friends. But the daily guidance and wisdom of my mom and dad helped ease the stress, steered me into good decisions, and I survived and ultimately thrived. I am full of gratitude for my parents and my high school experiences at Cardinal O'Hara.

***

I have many great and wonderful memories of my mother, something that is a blessing unto its own. She died in 2005 and we terribly miss her, of course, but the loss is lessened in that she truly lives on in our hearts and minds because of many indelible experiences and episodes she left with us. As I mentioned, growing up my mother was my biggest fan, and I obviously loved her a lot, too. Growing up as a young teen, I played baseball in one form or another, dawn to dusk—either at the local playground, in our backyard, or pitching against the public mailbox across the street. One particular day my mother decided that we all needed to begin doing chores, and my assigned chore was scrubbing the kitchen floor. And back then it was done the old fashioned way—a bucket of water, scrub brush, down on my knees. That night I had a baseball game and I hit a triple—my first triple ever! I was so excited I couldn't wait to go home and tell her! When I finally did, she replied: "That is so fantastic, but I have to tell you that you hit a home run in my heart today the way you scrubbed the kitchen floor." That was just one life example that taught me cleanliness means a lot in the Italian culture!

***

My mom had a way with words, phrases, or facial expression. She was what most people would call a character. And I mean that in a positive loving way. I just don't think people call me a "character" but rather terms like…"predictable," "methodical," "boring"? But not my mom. She had a distinct world view and numerous ways to convey that view.

She could be blunt: "You are such a BS-er," she blurted out one day when, fresh out of college, I was working on my resume.

"Mom! You are my mother, how can you say that to me?"

"Because I am reading over your resume here and you have not done half the things you claim here. Half of it is bull."

"Okay, maybe, but I have only been out of college a year and I just don't have that much to talk about so I need to exaggerate a little bit."

"A little bit? You just better hope nobody checks on these."

Okay—I deleted all my exaggerations and let honesty be the best policy. And looking back, it all worked out just fine.

Yes, when it came to her dealings with her precious family members there were no filters. She told you what she was thinking...as she was thinking...about whatever.

And often for emphasis, she would tilt her head to the side and mutter through clenched jaws as if nobody would hear her if she did this. One random example regarding baseball and religion comes to mind.

"This guy is easy pickings and will convert to anything. First the church and now the Phillies!"

That was her response when, after living in North Jersey for twenty years, I said, "I think it is time to convert from a Phillies fan to a Yankees fan." And the backstory is that I had been a lifelong Catholic and then in midlife, I began attending Protestant churches. She thought that I was a traitor on both counts. In my mind I was a Catholic Christian, then I was a Protestant Christian—but always a Christian. One emphasized the fear of God and the other emphasized the love of God. I thought a firm appreciation of both views was a solid foundation of faith. But apparently my mother had a different point of view. What is a son to do!

***

There were twelve years between me and my youngest sibling, Mark. You can do the math and see that for over the first decade of their marriage, my mother had little time for anything else other than nurturing newborns and tending to almost every other stage of child development. I cannot imagine the challenges. Think about it: when I was in seventh to eighth grade as a preteen, the youngest child was a newborn and in-between were toddlers and adolescents.

As a parent, how do you learn to do what you are supposed to do in each stage? It makes my head spin. How do you learn parenting? My mother was the next to youngest of seven siblings— five boys and two girls. So her parents had a lot of practice by the time they reached her. And her mother and father modeled for her—

what you might call the early twentieth-century unwritten Italian handbook for child-raising. Looking back and then returning to the present and comparing...you could do a lot worse. If I took a shot at categorizing what these childhood development principles were, it probably went something like this—we could call them the "Anna Cordivari 10 Commandments."

Anna Cordivari 10 Commandments

1. Family is first, foremost and always your top priority.
2. Your mother, father, brothers and sisters are the most important and dependable people in this world so treat them accordingly.
3. Wash your face, brush your teeth, make your bed, dress nice. Cleanliness is next to Godliness.
4. Be nice and polite to everyone. It is a reflection on your parents and your family name.
5. Eat everything I put on your plate and do not complain. Your father works hard to put food on the table.
6. Study hard and get good grades. Your parents did not raise dumb children. Don't complain about your teachers or how hard your tests are. Just work harder!

---

7. Get up, get dressed and go to church every Sunday. Because it is right or because I told you to. Either way...Just do it. And don't complain.

8. There is the contemporary expression, "I got your back." Meaning I am watching out for you. This was a teaching of my mother a long time ago. She would teach — You better have your family's back. Don't you ever let me see you siding with someone else against your brother or sister or family.

9. Yes, every weekend, you can count on going to some family member's birthday, Baptism, Holy Communion, anniversary, whatever. Because your family is most important. You may complain now but you will appreciate when you get older.

10. Don't talk back. Parenting is not a negotiation.

***

Mom was also a great and gracious cook. The regular menu included spaghetti, meatballs, Italian sausage, and her own special sauce—we called it "gravy" back then! Peppers and eggs on an Italian roll. Veal scallopini. Spaghetti with olive oil, bread crumbs or minced tuna during Lent. Meatloaf, steak, mashed potatoes. And a great "house salad" of iceberg, tomatoes, cucumbers, salt, pepper, olive oil, and vinegar which she would toss with her hands — claiming it was the secret ingredient. I have to admit that it was simple but perfecto!

There were also special dishes where she handed down her "secret recipe." One of the family favorites was her "scrippels," which is what she and my grandparents called them. It is an abridgment of *escrippels*, which is an Italian to English translation somehow of crepes. This was a special dish that we would have on Christmas, Easter, and during Lent — escarole soup with scrippels. The soup was chicken stock, carrots, onions, celery, and the spinach-like green, escarole. But this was just the background music to the main event of the scrippels. The recipe for a scrippel consisted of what I later termed the FEW recipe, as in flour, eggs, and water whipped to a paint-like consistency. Mom would demonstrate how you were to heat a griddle or large pan until it was hot enough that when you flicked a few beads of water, the beads would "dance" on the hot surface. Yes, I appreciated the passion and attention to detail that Mom brought to the kitchen. Once the crepes started to curl on the edges, they were done. You rolled them up into a lengthwise tube and set them aside. After you made about four dozen, the family of eight was ready to eat. You place three or four of the scrippels across a soup dish, add the hot escarole soup and ... Mangia!

And for dessert, there was always a fairly available production of chocolate cake with chocolate icing and jimmies. Another of my favorite chocolate desserts was what she called "icebox cake." It consisted of multiple layers of crumbled graham crackers interspersed with layers of chocolate pudding topped with the ultimate layer of crumbled graham crackers and then chilled in the refrigerator. In her parent's day, the refrigerator was called "the icebox" hence the name. I confess today to being an unabashed chocoholic. And to this day don't tell me it is called dessert if it does not include chocolate!

Years later in my adult years and living in the Northeast, Italian restaurants are all the rave. As a clueless and take-everything-for-granted kid growing up, I had no idea my house had a five-star Italian restaurant. Thank you, Mom!

Mom shared her great cooking with all of our friends as well. And we had a constant influx of male friends to our house. I specify *male* because I remember one time in my college years asking her if I could have a certain young lady I had dated a couple of times to be a guest for dinner. To my surprise, since we always seemed to have an open-door policy, Mom said, "No. I don't want to be making dinner for every one of your floozies. When you are serious about some girl, you can invite her to dinner." I was taken aback. Also, I had never heard the word "floozie" before and had to look it up. Dictionary definition of floozie: "a girl or a woman who has a reputation for promiscuity." I said, "Mom! What are you talking about!" Shook my head, left the room, and never broached the subject of a female guest again. Just another example of what a character Mom was.

***

The first house I remember growing up in was this tiny little box of three bedrooms and one bath on a quarter acre in Havertown, Pennsylvania. I attended kindergarten through eighth grade in that town, so I know I lived there at least nine years, which is the longest I have ever lived anywhere. As an adult, I have seen as common in our American culture the size of the house proclaiming your social status. I can look back and say that I was very happy in the smallest house in which I ever dwelled. As a kid I was oblivious to the fact that we had to be piled on top of one another. By eighth grade I was sharing a bedroom with Rich and Rob. Adrienne was in the second bedroom and I recall Bruce in a crib in her room. And my mom, dad, and "baby" Mark were in my parents' bedroom. I dare not call it a "master bedroom," but it did have the only bathroom in the house. How did we make it work? I think my mother could have lost her sanity at this point. She was likely close to her wit's end but she held it together until the year I graduated eighth grade and we moved to the "Big House" with its four bedrooms, two-and-a-half baths on a full acre. We were moving up. Praise the Lord!

We had a huge backyard for football and baseball games. There was a long driveway and a hoop that hosted at least a decade of neighborhood basketball games. And we had a large unfinished basement with cinderblock walls and wood-studded ceiling—perfect for teenage boys to bounce off the walls while doing minimum damage. With all of the above plus a pool table, ping pong table, and a dartboard, the new reality was...why go somewhere else?

My parents' strategy was probably along the lines of *We would rather put up with all the noise, clatter and clutter to go along with the tradeoff of knowing where you are, what you are doing, and who you are doing it with.* I remember basketball games out in the driveway going on until 10:30 at night as lights started to go out in surrounding homes and echoes of boys' shouts starting to reverberate against the silence. I don't recall neighbors ever complaining, probably because we were surrounded by families with teenagers and the parents were understanding.

Given that I was only two years older than next brother Rich and four years older than next brother Rob, we often had quite a large gathering of each one's friends. There could be some very large and long basketball tournaments or football marathons. When we were not at home, we were either at the nearby Garrett Hill playground grinding out the same sports or up at "the Field House." And by the Field House I mean the hallowed halls of the Villanova Field House where we were either watching the team play or practice, or we were sneaking in and playing until we got thrown out.

***

You can see that the Cordivari family was synonymous with sports. I give all credit to my dad. He was proficient at every sport. As a result, I think just about all of his children were. No, we were not superstars and rarely even varsity material—though some were. Our sister Adrienne made the women's varsity basketball team at Villanova as a 5'2" point guard! So proud of her achievement, we pat ourselves on the back and think growing up with five brothers had something to do with it! But we were all proficient in many sporting endeavors. Dad taught us all how to throw a pitch, a fastball, and a curve! ("You put your fingers here along the seams... you break your wrist just as you release... you keep the same motion for fastball and curve so you can throw off the batter's timing.) He taught us how to catch and bat. He taught us how to shoot a basketball and throw a spiral pass. He would come out and mix it up with all of us for a little while and then catching his breath, would say, "Okay, that's enough!" But I can see him getting home from work in his suit and white shirt, rolling up his sleeves for a quick game of H-O-R-S-E, or to try to toss a couple of touchdown passes before dinner. He also liked to tweak us and after he won at hoops or threw the touchdown pass, he would say with a twinkle in his eyes, "Did I tell you about the time I won the trophy for (fill in the blanks?)" And he was so humble and warm we knew he wasn't bragging. He was busting on us and we loved it.

Interestingly, the one sport he never taught us was golf. I did not pick up a club until I had graduated college and moved out of the house. And I never recall my father golfing when I was a teenager growing up. He had a demanding job all week as an aerospace engineer for a large corporation, and all the performance stress and time demands that go with that. Saturdays were for family, kids' sporting events, and home repairs. (As a mechanical engineer, he could fix anything, from cars to radios to a busted mailbox.) I remember a Saturday night ritual was taking a five-minute drive with him down to a large newsstand on City Line Avenue where he would get the just-published editions of the local Sunday papers. Why I remember it perhaps was that it was a milestone that the typical very busy Saturday was coming to an end. And my mother and father would enjoy the newspaper after the last child was tucked into bed.

***

But my memory was not totally accurate about when Dad played golf. He told me that he started playing golf when he was fourteen or fifteen years old when their house was near 65th Street and Vine in West Philadelphia. And there were two public golf courses nearby—Cobbs Creek and Karakung. He said that they would go and "mooch" balls and when you turned in a certain amount of balls, you got a club. It was a beat-up club somebody had lost or thrown in a pond, but it was a club. I should point out that this is a blue-collar working neighborhood in the early 1940's, so the country was in between coming out of a Depression and mobilizing for a world war.

But back to golf.

So he said with their handful of clubs and mooched balls, they would sneak on the course and play until they got caught and thrown off. When they were close to wearing out their welcome, they would pay the green fees that entitled you to unlimited golf and he said they would play all day until it was too dark. While he played scattered golf in high school, he said that he did not pick up a club during college—which is totally understandable, since for Dad college was a very serious time.

He was in a program called the V-12—which was essentially officer candidate school at a university level. The government paid for his college education which started at Drexel for a year, Bucknell for a year, and then Yale his last two years and from where he graduated. As a sidebar, I have this thing in my head about "Yale or Harvard" people. I think of all the presidents and government types and elites who attend these colleges for their pedigree, and then they tend to walk with a swagger and wear their Ivy League diploma on their sleeve. My dad is the furthest person from any of that. Dare I say...humble, modest, reserved. Consequently I just don't think or proclaim, "Hey, my dad went to Yale!" It just doesn't register. But since I have the topic on the table, how awesome it is that my dad went to Yale. Boolyah!!! Not only Yale but commissioned as an officer in the United States Marines. Ooohrah!

So this is why he did not play golf during college. He elaborated, saying, "I had to maintain a certain grade level because if I did not, I would be pulled out and most likely put on an express ship to Southeast Asia." WWII in the Pacific was in full bore during his college years. To wrap up the matter, he did not play golf; he did keep up his grades, graduated, and was commissioned. And just as he was graduating the war was winding down, so he was sent to Parris Island as a trainer/ administrator, never to leave the safe and sacred shores of the USA. He will often say, "This is one of many times when I know my God was looking out for me."

He said that he started playing golf again in 1973 when he worked at the Lansdale, Pennsylvania, plant of Philco-Ford and he played in a company golf league. Since he was born in 1925, that would make him forty-eight or thereabouts when he started playing regularly again. I did not remember him playing golf on the weekends but he told me, "No, I played regularly on Saturdays with your uncles or some longtime buddies from West Philadelphia. Your mother never complained and she was fine with it. Heck, I was home by 10:00 AM. We would go down and get in line at 4:00 AM, get our name on the board, leave our bags, and go to a diner and have breakfast. It was a lot of fun and I looked forward to it."

***

Sitting down to a family dinner every night with all of us at the table was a valued custom in our house. Many a night my dad's boss would call in the middle of dinner to discuss some manufacturing or logistics problem that needed his attention. Dad would handle his boss and then rejoin us for dinner. Those moments left lasting developmental impressions. Later on as an adult, I struggled like most with juggling work and family demands. But I learned from my dad you just have to get it done. Do your best and become a good juggler. There is no easy recipe except to commit to excellence in both realms. He was focused on the family and then the phone call would draw him back to the job. Then it was back to the family, finish dinner, help with homework, get the kids to bed, and then a quick preparation for the job tomorrow. Back to wife and newborn. Bedtime. Alarm goes off, out the door to the job and providing for the family. My dad taught us all an extremely valuable lesson for our careers and our marriages—it can be done! Not easy, but you will figure it out!

As mentioned, Dad tended towards optimism and Mom towards pessimism. Mom would say things like, "Everyone is a crook," "Show me a great fortune and I will show you a great crime," "Everyone is out to get you," or "You will never get a fair chance because you are Italian."

On this last thought, she had me rattled because I had set a goal of becoming very successful in business and I did not want to think my Italian surname was going to hold me back. So I pondered and thought that I would change my name from Cordivari to McCord. When I shared my thinking with my dad, in his very calm manner he said something along the lines of: "You could but your grandfather would disown you". Yikes! That sounded severe. My grandfather was my hero. I decided to keep the Cordivari name and take my chances.

But while my mother definitely leaned toward pessimism, I still learned many valuable life lessons from her. Her constant messages were about "You can do it; don't let them deny you; if you don't want to think that everybody is out to get you, at least be aware that when it comes to money and business, every smiling face is not necessarily a friend."

My mom was an amazing woman with incredible innate wisdom and a point of view on everything. She read widely, including books, magazines and newspapers, and she watched the news regularly. She never went to college but she was exceptionally smart, with a solid combination of intelligence and common sense or street smarts. She was a wizard with *New York Times* crossword puzzles. I was the college grad with a master's degree to boot, and yet I might get just one or two words figured out. She would complete it every day! In addition to this Italian-American woman having a mastery of the English language, she was well informed on all current affairs.

***

My mother had an interesting relationship with money. Born in 1924, she was a product of the Great Depression that had the country in its grip in the late 1920s and early 1930s. She was a very good steward of the family money, and I doubt she ever heard that term or thought about it applying to her. And this was yet another aspect of where, as the spouse, she was in great partnership with my dad. While Dad made the money, Mom managed it, stretching a dollar as far as possible and never wasting any of it.

She was the Queen of Coupons. She amassed coupons from the newspapers, magazines, mail circulars, and store handouts. She cut them out, categorized them, and put them into small envelopes. She never paid full price. And she "spread her wealth" around. She would mail out specific ones to her children, grandchildren, and daughters-in-law. If you had a cat, she would send you cat food coupons. Dog? You got dog food coupons. Baby in the house? You received the diaper coupons.

She would be appalled at some of our spending habits. Buying dish detergent at the local convenience store? Are you kidding me? You are paying 50 percent higher than waiting for the food store with a coupon. Going out to dinner? Rarely. She liked to cook. She knew she was a good cook. And she could put a five-star meal on the table for 20 percent of what a restaurant would charge. Why go out to a restaurant? In my parents' day, you took the family out to a restaurant on Easter, special birthdays, and anniversaries. It was not like today where eating out is the norm and eating a home-prepared meal is the exception.

New furniture? Renovations? Modernize the kitchen? No, not in my mom and dad's world. If it is not broken, why replace it? If you do not need to spend the money, then why spend the money? Family vacations? I think we went to Niagara Falls one time and Watkins Glen in upstate New York another. But otherwise, vacation was our family's designated week in the summer at the "Ventnor House." My grandfather, the immigrant who only completed sixth grade, was successful enough in the real estate, banking, and insurance business to be able to afford a second house on the bay in Ventnor, New Jersey not far from Atlantic City. We loved and treasured this simple but awesome week of family fun and togetherness at the Ventnor House.

So the point I am making is that my mother was very tight on controlling spending. Yet I am sure that I speak for all of my siblings in saying that we never felt poor or deprived. To the contrary, I felt like I had more than most of my friends and we certainly never went without something we needed. We were always dressed nicely — if not necessarily fashionably. And yes, I can say a little smugly looking backwards, being the firstborn of six means you never have to worry about wearing hand-me-downs, which was the common practice in our house for others!

The last word to say in speaking of my Mom and her relationship with money is ... casino. After the kids were grown and out of college, my mom, who had nursed nickels all those years, emerged as this new woman. She enjoyed going to the Atlantic City casino a couple times a month. My mom would play the slot machines, quarters and nickels. There were not many nickel slots but she would find them. She started to amass these large buckets of nickels and quarters at home. And she was now accumulating valued customer points at the hotels complete with room upgrades and comped meals. I was starting to get alarmed and said to her one time, "Mom, you are not blowing all of my inheritance money, are you?" She replied, "Darn right I am! Your father and I provided for you all while you were growing up and now we are living it up!" Okay, I said, and I assured her that I just wanted to make sure she and Dad were financially secure. "Don't worry about us—we are fine." My father said, "Oh yeah, we are fine." I found out later that my folks were more than fine. They raised six kids, put them all through Villanova plus two years at Old Dominion at full freight, no scholarships...and still had a nice nest egg left over. They were great managers of money with an ethos of responsibility and delayed gratification that you rarely see today.

***

I spent the majority of my career at Johnson and Johnson, which I often viewed as a leadership development factory. And I certainly believe that I benefited in this regard. However, much of leadership development is modeling. Who were your bosses, mentors, role models? In this regard, I truly believe that growing up in our formative years, my siblings and I had the best teachers, mentors, and role models in the world—our parents! They taught us the value of common sense and how to treat people with respect. It was a solid preparation for taking our place in the world.

God and Golf Moment

Play by the Rules!

God has rules. Golf has rules. God gave us the Ten Commandments plus many other laws for living a righteous life contained throughout the Bible. Golf has the "Rules of Golf," a lengthy work with many elaborate details about the do's and don'ts of the game.

Jesus said, "Obey my commandments." No false gods. No taking the Lord's name in vain. Keep Sunday holy. Cherish your parents. Do not kill. Do not cheat on your spouse. Do not steal. Do not lie. Do not covet your neighbor's wife or property.

The commonality of the rules in both God's world and the golf world is to maintain integrity, fairness, and discipline. And the rules are also intended to protect us from ourselves. That is, to protect us from our broken, lazy selves always looking for the shortcut. And unfortunately there are usually pain and consequences that result from the shortcut.

Those who disregard the discipline of learning the rules, whether of God or golf, usually incur a slow frustrating journey of stunted growth and repeating the same flawed acts again and again.

Self-deception is at the center of fudging the score or rationalizing our sin. Learning to play by the rules is truly in our best interest and the faster way to growth and proficiency.

Chapter 3

THE PATRIARCH

> *"Leave your country, your people and your father's household and go to the land I will show you. I will make you into a great nation and I will bless you. I will make your name great and you will be a blessing."*
>
> *- Genesis 12:1–2*

William Anthony Cordivari was many things, but above all he was considered a gentleman. I can vouch for that assessment because I was his grandson and loved to spend time with him. My grandfather was nine years old when his family immigrated to the United States from Teramo, Italy, in 1911.

"Pretty good for a guy who never went past sixth grade," he would like to tease me. "Grandpop" was a very hardworking individual who personified the American Dream. He had to overcome many challenges to become a successful businessman. A limited education, learning a new language, and being viewed as a stranger in a foreign land could not stop him. He was a self-employed entrepreneur with an insurance agency and real-estate business. He learned through successes and failures with both good and bad partners. He succeeded in creating a business, a livelihood, and an excellent reputation. He and his wife, Jennie, had four children. These children of immigrants had the opportunity to go to college. My dad went to Yale, a source of pride for Grandpop.

The secrets of my grandfather's success were fairly straight-forward. He worked long and hard, plus he cared about people. His appearance was very professional. He was about five feet six or seven, medium build, and very trim. I often thought that his diet was salad, caffeine, and nicotine. He was a chain-smoker and his voice had that distinct gravelly sound to it. He had thick gray hair and a widow's peak slicked back in a very dapper sort of way. His eyes were green with a sparkling and engaging way about them. It seemed he was always in a three-piece suit with cuff links. When he wore an overcoat he also wore a hat, which he would tug and adjust to a perfect position on his head.

He became president of the West Philadelphia Board of Realtors and in later life worked for a large corporate real-estate firm. But it was not his success that distinguished him; it was his caring and polite nature. He was a widower the last twenty-five years of his life. He filled this void by focusing his attention on his children and grandchildren until he died at the age of ninety-two.

As a young man, I dabbled in local politics and went door-to-door securing votes in my neighborhood. I will never forget this elderly lady who greeted me through the crack of her door. "I am Bill Cordivari, candidate for township commissioner, and I am seeking your vote."

She looked me over. In a frail voice she said, "Are you related to the Bill Cordivari who ran the real-estate business in Philadelphia?"

"Yes, he is my grandfather," I replied.

"Well, if you are half the gentleman he was, you get my vote, sonny."

I thanked her and walked away with a new understanding about what really mattered in life. And I was very proud that William Anthony Cordivari was my grandpop.

My great grandfather was Davide Cordivari, and he lived from 1871–1933. He was born and raised in the Teramo/Abruzzi part of Italy near Rome. In 1902, he and his family migrated to the United States. He settled in Bryn Mawr, Pennsylvania. We do not know the exact address but given his immigrant status, it is very likely he was living on "the other side of the tracks." I do know exactly where Railroad Avenue is, the mythical dividing line between the haves and have-nots. And we are not certain but it was either the Overbrook Country Club or Merion Golf Club where he worked as a greenskeeper tending to the plush fairways and greens of a private club. He likely walked or rode a bicycle to work since automobiles were scarce in those days.

I find it fascinating that my great grandfather who I only recently learned about had a connection to golf. I can only imagine, given what I have read about the turn of the century in our country, that he was likely not welcome to play the course, let alone even think of membership. So I want to thank him belatedly and posthumously for coming to this country breaking the barriers so that a hundred years later his great grandson could not only play but even join some of the most spectacular golf clubs anywhere.

I have very little knowledge of my maternal grandparents on the Liberi side, as they both died when I was a youngster. Funny but I only have one memory and I had to be five or six. My grandparents lived in West Philadelphia in a row house with a tiny backyard. I was sitting at the kitchen table and my grandmother was preparing dinner, shucking peas out of the pods. She taught me how to do it and I was able to help her. I also remember that looking right out the back door was a single peach tree in the middle of this postage-stamp yard and we went and picked some peaches off the tree. And my grandfather made his own wine in the basement, which was common, I imagine, of immigrants living on small incomes.

I do have one memory of Grandpop Liberi, and that was of him taking me by the hand and we walked a few blocks to the local Italian-American club. And there behind the walls men sat at tables drinking small glasses of red wine as they played checkers, and tossed bocci balls. That is it. Those are the memories of a child. I wonder if they are true or if I made them up or if I jumbled them with other family events. It doesn't really matter. My testimony is harmless to all and pleasurable to me. So it has become my reality.

One last point and it is not minor. I do remember both Grandmom and Grandpop Liberi as wonderfully loving and doting grandparents. Given the Italian culture, I would be shocked if I was making this up! But it is a critical core of my life. I had parents and two sets of grandparents who surrounded me, protected me, and encouraged me with their boundless unconditional love. What a gift—and as I have grown up, come to realize what a rare gift. But I believe that whatever success I have had in career or love or family has sprung from the foundation of this priceless gift of parental love.

My paternal grandparents on the Cordivari side lived 10 minutes away and we saw them all the time. What a blessing that was. Often I would take a bus from school to Grandpop's real estate office and hang around while he finished up. Then we would head home to his house for dinner and we might even cruise past a house for an appraisal. My grandmother would welcome me with a big smile, a hug, and say, "Here is my grandson the doctor." Yes, I had said that I would like to be a doctor. And that became to anyone my grandmother came in contact with as "my grandson the doctor."

As a child and youth, I loved going over to their house for dinner. My grandmother was a great cook of the Italian immigrant tradition. And she always made my favorite dessert—chocolate cake, with chocolate icing and multicolored jimmies on top.

My grandparents were awesome in many dimensions, but the key was probably the unlimited and unabashed love they showered on their grandkids and the obvious joy they exuded in our presence. I never take for granted that I won life's lottery by being born into a family wherein parents and grandparents and extended family of aunts and uncles surround you with their love. I have the highest regard for people who are born into very tough if not outright hazardous family conditions and still make something very positive out of their life.

My grandmother, Jennie Cordivari, died from a rare, barely understood disease when I was a sophomore in college. It is amazing that in that relatively short time we spent together, I still have so many fond memories and stories locked away in my heart and soul. Her love lives on forever.

My grandfather lived to ninety-two, so I had him in my life a lot longer and he even got to see his great grandchildren. And oh, how he loved them. They called my dad "pop-pop" and they referred to William A. as "pop-pop-pop."

I remember a particular story towards the end of his life very clearly. He was in the hospital and our son Andrew had just been born. I went to the hospital with my father to see my grandpop. He apparently had become somewhat cantankerous the last couple of days—withdrew from people and stopped eating—and it was a difficult situation. I could see that it was wearing on my dad. He said to my grandfather, "Dad, you want to get up? Bill is here." I think he just pulled the covers up. "Dad, don't you want something to eat? You have not eaten in days?" From under the covers, "No!" My dad asked me, "Do you have that photo of Andrew with you?" It was a photo of our newborn taken in the hospital about a week earlier. "Yes", I said. "Let me have it," my father said. He took the photo, stuck it under the covers in my grandfather's face, and said, "Dad, look— your newest great-grandchild." After a couple of seconds, the covers came flying, my grandfather sprang up to a sitting position, hair disheveled, no glasses on, and exclaimed, *"He's beautiful!"* as he held Andrew's photo. What an awesome moment, and I was so grateful to my dad for his persistence.

My grandfather died a couple of years later. He was a blessed man. He lived a long life, had a lot of children, grandchildren, great grandchildren. He was successful, loved, and gave love.

***

When Grandpop died, I was a little down as I approached his funeral Mass, and not just because it was a funeral. I was at a foggy place in my faith at the time in the sense that I would worry about who was going to heaven or not. As if I had been given this grand insight. So I was worried about my grandfather because as kind and as wonderful as he was, I never heard him say anything about his faith. My grandmother seemed to be the faithful or religiously compliant one of the family.

So at Grandpop's funeral, it was a joy and a relief to hear the priest talk about the frequent visits he had with my grandfather over the last few weeks of his life. The priest spoke of how he visited Grandpop every day and brought him communion. And he went on and on about how much Grandpop loved Jesus. "Oh, how he loved Jesus." Wow. I didn't see that coming. Who would know? Grandpop was part of an earlier generation. No hugs. Feelings kept under wraps. He loved me. I loved him. But the name Jesus never came up. "Judge not lest you be judged." I was relieved and reassured that I would see my grandfather again in eternity.

One of the great leaders of the Bible, Abraham, had been promised blessings beyond his comprehension. He is recognized as the root of the Jewish, Muslim, and Christian faiths. I am sure old Abraham never saw that coming. How many billions of offspring sprung forth from Abraham? It is difficult to calculate over the ages.

But I started thinking about Grandfather William A. one day. He had four children. My father had six. I have five. My children have produced six grandchildren thus far. Just in my family line, that is twenty-one. If I go to the official family tree and count everyone who sprang from Grandpop, it is over fifty and growing exponentially by the year. What a legacy! What a contribution to humanity. What a life of meaning. It makes my head spin.

God and Golf Moment

Loosen Your Grip

There is an instinctual behavior in golf to try to control everything too much, and this is particularly true with the golf swing.

The tendency is to squeeze the club very tight in an attempt to increase control. But in reality, all that does is tighten the muscles in the hands, arms and shoulders, and results in poor outcomes. What works much better is to loosen your grip (counterintuitive) and let the club swing. Just let the laws of physics kick in and then watch some beautiful shots.

Life is the same.

We say we believe in God and trust in God, but then we try to overcontrol events and situations most if not all of the time and self-defeat the power of the Holy Spirit inside us. To make life easier, "loosen your grip" on things and let God have control. As is said, "Let go. Let God."

Chapter 4

CALLED TO FAITH

"For many are called but few are chosen."
                                    - Matthew 22:14

I can honestly say, both while looking back and what I felt at the time, my childhood up until high school was heaven on earth. I was a totally happy and confident little boy and then emerging young man. I was born into a family of great parents, grandparents, and endless aunts, uncles, cousins, and other relatives living nearby. My four brothers and sister are to this day very close. We lived in a great middle-class neighborhood about two blocks from the playground where all day we played baseball, football, or climbed the playground equipment. We hiked around the woods and streams. I had a roof over my head, food in my belly, and lots of kids my age nearby. We walked or rode our bikes to school which was about six blocks away. Summing it all up, what not to like?

And we were also a strong family of faith. That was part of the growing-up experience. We all attended Catholic grade school and we went to church every Sunday. As an aside I certainly took it for granted, but can you imagine what a herculean effort was required every Sunday to get six kids bathed, dressed, and fed to get out the door to church? The degree of difficulty is extreme. It is like so many aspects of parenting. When you are the kid and it is being done to you by your parent, it looks so easy. When you are the parent doing it to the kid or the kids, it gets reduced to ... *God, give me the strength to get through this task or this day.*

Reflecting back on my early childhood experiences regarding my faith, one story that stands out is that I would play "Mass" up in my bedroom of our very small house. The details were sketchy to me, but I ran them past two of my brothers. Rich confirmed that I did indeed play Mass. And Rob was quick to add, "And you were a good priest! Nothing weird going on." Thanks, guys.

I was an altar boy in Catholic grade school (now referred to as "elementary school.") I think I liked all the trappings of being a priest and saying Mass in a large but peaceful and beautiful church. Way back then there was something appealing about the quietness of early morning as I headed out to serve at 6:30 AM Mass during the week. It was dark outside and the votive candles lit the inside. The priest spoke in hushed tones and in Latin. I liked the vestments, the outer garments, the colors changing with the various liturgical seasons—

Advent, Christmas, Lent, Easter, Pentecost, etc. So I would use a different color towel as my cape to match the season. I liked the shiny gold chalice and the pallet or protective square that went on top of it. The Bible and Church Missile with all the multicolored ribbons hanging out were cool, I thought. I had a similar book at home given to me as a student. I tried to recreate as much of the church Mass experience complete with conscripting my younger brothers to be my altar boys whether they wanted to or not. Very Catholic indeed!

I recited all of the above to highlight the fact many elements of my faith were taking root as I was a young child. I had respect for authority figures — parents, priests, police, military. At this point, I was just this happy naive young kid.

***

Up until freshman year of high school, I thought life was perfect and near paradise on earth. I had loving parents, great sibs, cool neighborhood, lots of fun and games. Additionally, I was surrounded by a great big extended Italian family of grandparents, cousins, aunts and uncles. They all lived nearby and we saw each other regularly. We had parties, christenings, gatherings in the park, and hanging out at the Jersey shore.

At age fourteen, death seemed like a theoretical distant concept. I remember something said at school triggered deep thoughts. Death? Yes, I guess it is real because one of my grandparents died so I knew death was real on one plane. But it pertained to other people. For me, it seemed like a thousand years off. It was so far off that I could not grasp it, so I put it out of my mind and headed for a wiffle ball game with my buddies.

But that chapter of my life—call it idyllic naiveté or living in a protected bubble—came crashing down on November 22, 1963, the day that President John F. Kennedy was assassinated. I was walking down the hall at school and three girls passed me. Initially I thought they were laughing (and I assumed that they were laughing at me.) But they were not laughing, they were crying. Shortly we were all gathered in our classrooms and the principal made the announcement over the public address system that President Kennedy had been shot in Dallas. Soon there was another announcement confirming that he was dead.

I recall being sad, shocked, upset and scared. I was very scared. What vile dark evil force was unleashed in the world? My president was dead. My young, cool, funny, athletic president was dead. Murdered with his brains splattered all over his wife's pink dress and the back of the car, and captured on live TV amid continuous replay. How could anyone alive that day forget that image? I was both scared and scarred. The event changed me permanently in many different ways. First, it put Evil right in my face where I could not miss it. In a world of good and evil, up until now I only knew and had only experienced good. Second, it spurred me to ask the question: where was God in the midst of this horror? And at the time, as a young teenager early in my faith walk, I did not have an answer. That made me scared, angry, and cynical. Over the next twenty to twenty-five years, people would oft comment something along the lines of ... "Bill, you are so sarcastic ... or cynical." This is also the period I would describe as wandering in my spiritual wilderness. My education contained a fairly heavy dose of religion and spirituality, but I was walking or drifting away from it.

It was not just the Kennedy assassination in 1963. Vietnam was raging between 1964–1973, which fell square in the middle of my high school and college years. There was a military draft to fuel the needs for soldiers to fight overseas. A lottery was created by birth date. My number was 2! I was likely shipping out after college or so I thought. Layer on top of this, Martin Luther King was assassinated in April 1968 and Robert F. Kennedy in June 1968. Admittedly the country was reeling and so was I.

Whereas the first fourteen years of my life were like paradise on earth, the next ten years — while still surrounded by a loving family — was playing out against a social and political backdrop of the Kingdom of Hell unleashed on earth. How could my worldview and spiritual beliefs not be impacted by all of this? Thoughts went through my head like, *Who is God? What is God? What kind of God reigns over all of this mayhem?* I would find reasonable answers to these tough questions later in life as my faith walk would progress and strengthen, but it was messing with my mind and spirit as a young lad. I clearly drifted away from God during my college years, but looking back many years later I could clearly see that God never drifted away from me or let go of his grip on me.

High school was heavy on faith and family and nil on fairways. College was a time of separating from God, separating from family, and golf was still nonexistent in my life. I never played golf in high school or college; I was first introduced to it right after college. I had enlisted in the Army Reserve and had to serve six months active duty right after college graduation. I was in Fort Lewis, Seattle, for basic training. When we finally got a weekend pass after what seemed like forever, the guys I was hanging with decided we would get a motel room, play cards, drink beer, and play a round of golf. I recall thinking that the game was very hard, but we had fun and when you unwittingly ignore half the rules of golf and then declare yourself a decent score, it is not nearly as humbling or demoralizing as it can be.

Upon graduation from college with a degree in biology, I now had to find a job. At the conclusion of my active duty service in the military, I had reserve commitments every month and summers for the next six years. But it was a deal I had agreed to, and I strived to do my best in this endeavor while there was still a lot of social strife going on around the Vietnam War, even though American "boots on the ground" was winding down.

***

In terms of my faith walk, I was now entering what I later referred to as the "wilderness years." The time in the wilderness included seeking direction, meaning, and purpose—looking for a job, trying to establish who I was and what I would become. But I was going to do it alone my way. I did not need God. I stopped going to church now that I was out in the world making my own decisions. One of those choices was that I would play golf on Sundays. The little voice would whisper, *You should be in church*, but my loud voice replied, *I like it better out here on the golf course. I am surrounded by God's beautiful creation. Let me worship by being out here instead.* It would be many years before I became a regular church attendee again, finding time elsewhere during the week to work in golf.

God and Golf Moment

Take a Mulligan!

A "Mulligan" is a term used in casual golf when someone wants a "do over." This is invoked after someone has hit a really bad shot. They usually shout out an expletive or some other form of grumbling and try to explain away their misfire. And then they might say, "I am taking a Mulligan." And what this really means is ... don't count that last shot ... I am taking another shot. It may make one feel good in the moment. It favorably improves the score but does not accurately reflect or record actual golfing ability. But if it is just fun golf with the gang, no worries, take a Mulligan.

In professional golf, there are no Mulligans. The professional golfer lives and dies on every shot, good, bad, ugly. And they must record every shot and their overall score for posterity and all the world to see.

In casual golf, there are Mulligans. In professional golf—no Mulligans.

But guess what? In matters of faith and life ... the important things, Jesus gives you a Mulligan! We are initially condemned by our sin but if we accept Jesus as Savior and Lord and profess our faith in his life, death and resurrection, we are assured of eternal life. (John 3:16.) We get a do-over.

"For God so loved the world that he gave his only begotten son. And all who believe in him shall not perish but have eternal life."

Chapter 5

LOVE AND MARRIAGE

"And we know that in all things God works for the good of those who love him who have been called according to his purpose."
- Romans 8:28

I met Cyndee in a one-in-a-million coincidence when we were seated together on a 35-minute flight from Pittsburgh to Newark. I later learned that with God in control, there are no coincidences. But I would often think... what if we were in different aisles or off by one seat... or different flights the same night? Who can understand the finest details on which momentous life shifts hinge? When I cannot understand, I fall back on Romans 8:28 above. We just have to trust that somehow God is working in unseen ways. He even takes our brokenness and maneuvers circumstances to produce good in ways we could never fathom.

In any event, over the next few months we dated, courted, and decided we would get married. I was very nervous when I went to meet Cyndee's father to ask for his daughter's hand in marriage. I was previously married and not sure how he was going to react to that. In fact, it went very well and we had very good discussions. He was and is a great gentleman, soft spoken, wise yet humble, with a resolute iron backbone when it comes to his belief, witnessing or defending his faith.

"How did it go?" asked Cyndee. I said, "It went really well. Your dad is a great guy, though he does seem very religious." I was not sure what I was trying to say with the last sentence. "He is not really religious but he is a committed Christian," she said. *Hmmm … committed Christian …* I never heard that term before. It would be a few years later under the influence of my wife, her dad, her sister, my new church, pastor, and Bible study that I began the transition to get to the place where I would be proud and humbled to be known as a *committed Christian.* Or "C-squared" as my friend calls it.

***

Two years later, we were married in a small ceremony in Union, South Carolina, the town where her parents lived. After our honeymoon in Charleston and Asheville, we moved to Bedminster, New Jersey. We were essentially starting anew. Early on, Cyndee said that she really liked the church she was leaving behind in Pittsburgh and it was important that we find a good church in New Jersey.

One day Cyndee saw a blurb in the local paper that a new pastor, Steve McConnell, had been assigned to a local church. Cyndee said that she knew him from attending the same college. "Let's go hear him preach," she said. So we did. Everything connected between Pastor Steve, who reached out and supported my growing faith along with the church, the people, and the location. That is how we became members of Liberty Corner Presbyterian Church and, over twenty-five years later, we are still members. This one event of stepping out in faith would subsequently continue to open one beneficial door after another.

***

Cyndee and I were blessed with children. But before we had children, we had heartbreak in the form of a miscarriage and a strange related medical development known as trophoblastic disease. It is rare in occurrence and has the potential for a deadly outcome. It was bad enough when the doctor told us that the baby had stopped growing, but then he said there was evidence of this rare condition where the fetal tissue grows outside the uterus. It struck me as similar to cancer ... cells growing where they should not. We were both devastated. We had only been married for two years and joyfully married. The thought that my wife could be snatched away by a cruel turn of fate sent me into a dark place, an abyss. On Cyndee's side, she said tearfully, "This is not how I thought things were going to turn out for us. But I have to trust in God. I am going up to bed." I was trying to process this statement as my longtime faith was actually a fledgling faith up to now. I asked her respectfully and with as much empathy as I could muster if she would mind if I stayed downstairs. I told her that I just needed to think and pray and stare into space. I was overwhelmed and did not know where to turn. She said that she understood.

So on this particular night after receiving the bad news and worse news from our doctor, I was slumped on our living room floor, my back up against the sofa staring into space. I decided to turn on our old stereo which was preloaded with eight CDs and I couldn't tell you who or what except I know that they were all classical music CDs to which I had started listening as a form of relaxation. Quick but relevant backstory: when we joined Liberty Corner Presbyterian Church, I stepped into the many customs and cultures of a "Reformed" vs. Catholic Church, and that included a lot of different hymns that had become imbedded into Sunday worship. My newfound favorite was Hymn #1 in the hymnal, "Joyful, Joyful, We Adore Thee." It is such a beautiful hymn with praise to a loving God with pure poetry in the verses. And there is a beautiful melody that goes with the verses. This backdrop is important to the story.

After staring into the darkness with my head spinning, my stomach churning and no resolutions coming into focus, I decided to turn on the stereo hoping the music might calm me. I had not turned the stereo on in weeks and had no idea where the rotation was. So it was a shock, a beautiful shock to my system, when the first music I heard was the melody from Hymn #1, "Joyful, Joyful We Adore Thee." I had no idea the melody was written by Beethoven and that the CD that was "randomly" playing by "coincidence" was Beethoven's Ninth Symphony, "Ode to Joy." As my mind and soul calculated it all, I wept as I felt the arms of an all-loving God enveloping me in my darkest moment when I most needed it. I felt a peace that I never experienced before and found difficult to explain. Years later as my faith matured, I learned that there are no random events or coincidences with a loving God who meets the needs of the faithful believers. I would read in the book of Isaiah in the Bible,

"When you pass through the waters, I will be with you; and when you pass through the rivers, they will not sweep over you. When you walk through the fire, you will not be burned; the flames will not set you ablaze."

We got through the fire with God's gracious covering of peace, patience, and understanding. Over the next five years two successful pregnancies produced two more awesome children, Andrew and Raquel, adding on to the wonders of Billy, Jackie, and Matt who are a blessing to all.

Cyndee became the root from which many flourishing vines sprang. Examples: our children obviously. Our church of many years and the people from our church who led me to my Friday morning Men's Bible Study, which I have been attending for over twenty-five years now.

She suggested Mountain Air. More on this beautiful patch of earth later.

When it was clear that my twenty-three-year run at Johnson & Johnson was coming to an end and I needed my next job, she suggested I meet with the husband of her friend she had met at the church Women's Bible study. This fellow knew the CEO who subsequently hired me to a senior commercial position. And from my six years in this job, I met executives who would become my next two employers. All coming from the same root — my wife.

Cyndee is a very loving person, constantly thinking of what others need and particularly her family. She has a talent for buying gifts that meet the moment. One such story left me forever grateful to this day.

***

It was Father's Day weekend. I remember all of the details by what was going on at work. We had been married for two years and for her, me, and my children, we were all still working through the challenges of a blended family. That is why this present had so much personal meaning to me.

Billy, Jackie, and Matt had given me a golf shirt for Father's Day. It meant a lot to me coming from them. It was a white shirt with some red and blue stripe or pattern to it. That was Sunday. The following day I was playing at a corporate golf outing at the nearby Fiddlers Elbow Golf Club. I was in a great mood. Beautiful weather, no work, golf! And I was wearing my brand-new golf shirt.

I remember nothing about the golf that day except that it was a spectacular day. What came next was a bit annoying. In the locker room as scores of men were walking around in various stages of undress, toweled or butt naked, I ran into some colleagues and our conversation quickly shifted from golf to a continuation of a simmering work problem from the previous day. And I did not like the decisions that had been made without my input in another golf cart during the round! Well, this ruined what up to now had been a perfectly fine day. My mind was simmering. We showered, dressed, and sat down for a long obligatory dinner. I arrived home late and as I was emptying my gym bag, I discovered that my newly acquired and beloved golf shirt was missing! I looked in my bag and car a half dozen times. Noooooo! I was devastated. In the midst of my locker room distraction, I left the shirt behind. I awakened Cyndee and explained it to her. She suggested going back to the club early the next day to see if anyone had found it.

So I got to the club bright and early and explained my predicament to the locker room attendant. He showed me his lost and found pile and my shirt was not there. He said to me, "The only thing I can suggest to you is to go through the towels and see if it got swept up in them." Okay, I was excited. Maybe I would find it. But ... but then he took me around the corner and pointed. What did I see? Before me were hundreds and hundreds of wet dirty towels sitting in a mountain about to be picked up by laundry. I did not know whether to be happy or sad. (Side story: my family knows and they find it a source of kidding and jabbing me because ... true confession ... I don't like to get my hands dirty. Don't like dirty, gooey, sticky, and definitely not wet moldy towels. But this was a BIG deal and the clock was ticking.) File it under: The Things You Do for Love! So I rolled up my sleeves (dress shirt, suit and tie in those days) and started picking through one wet gross dank smelly towel after another until I had moved the entire mountain from one side of the room to the other and NO SHIRT! I was crestfallen and defeated. I was sad. I called home and gave Cyndee the update.

I headed out to work, had a full day, and then drove home. I met Cyndee at the door, kissed her hello, and then proceeded upstairs to change clothes before dinner. I had been sad and angry about the lost golf shirt all day—when what to my wonderment do I see? Yes, a brand-new exact replacement of the lost shirt lying on the bed. She had made it a point to go to the mall and see if she could find it, which she did. I was so happy on multiple fronts, but mainly feeling surrounded by the love of my children and the love of my wife. The lost golf shirt is in my family love highlights film. Oh, what a blessed man I am!

God and Golf Moment

Let Jesus Be Your Caddie

In professional golf, the caddie walks alongside the golfer.

The caddie carries the heavy bag and knows all the nuances of the golf course. The caddie knows the distances to the hole, where all the hazards are, where to shoot, and what to avoid. The caddie cleans the ball and equipment, plus keeps a constant supply of water and energy bars. He is a voice of encouragement to the pro when the pro may be struggling under the intense competition. The competitive pro would be at a distinct disadvantage without a caddie to help out in all of these areas.

Life can be very tough if you seek to go it alone. Let Jesus be your caddie.

Let him carry your burdens. Let him show you the way. Jesus said, *"Come all ye who are weary and burdened and I will give you rest."* Jesus can lighten our load, warn us of hazards to avoid, and just make the journey a lot more joyous like it was originally intended.

Chapter 6

BLESSED BY CHILDREN

"Let the little children come to me and do not hinder them, for the kingdom of God belongs to such as these."

- Mark 10:14

Thinking of children and where the faith, family, and fairways connections overlap ... I think of pork loin. Yes, pork loin. I will come back to it, so hold the thought.

Teenage boys are big eaters. At least the three that I raised and the four brothers with whom I grew up. And teenage daughters are the sweetest of God's creation the way they love their daddies. At least the two I raised and my sister. Those are my significant conclusions over two generations of family life.

My two older sons, Bill and Matt, both grew to about 6'3" and 200-plus pounds bulked up from weights and athletics. The amounts of food they have been observed to eat are biblical. Both played on a high-school lacrosse team that went to the state finals. Matt's team won the New Jersey state finals.. A *big deal!* And while I am on a roll, I should mention that daughter Jackie was captain of her high school soccer team. Proud father bragging a bit? Yes. Guilty as charged! But back to the food...

If we had the "big kids" — as we called the three older children over for dinner, Cyndee would be known to fret, "Did I make enough food for Billy?" The answer was usually no! The big kids still had big appetites but we loved it. We had a big house with a long dining room table, and we had many a love fest around that table which continued as the "big kids" married and their wonderful spouses joined us as well.

***

A few words on birth order, family dynamics, and parenting are in order. In a family of six children, if my parents did malpractice along the way, I was oblivious to it. But when it is you who are the parent, there is a different perspective. Bill was my firstborn. How scary to be twenty-something and a parent for the first time. I was not even sure if we were allowed to give him water when we got him home from the hospital. (Nurse: "Of course you can give him water. You can't live without water, silly.") I mention that just to say that you don't know beans when you are a young parent for the first time. I felt inadequate, guilty, unsure making on-the-spot "do that or don't do that" decisions. Particularly with a firstborn son, we had the whole alpha male dynamics to work through. I was the alpha male in the house. He was the emerging alpha male. (Somewhere in the teenage years, I recall the incident of seeing double after his elbow came down on my head as we were contesting a rebound while playing basketball in the driveway. I knew then that I had crossed a certain threshold. The passing of the guard!)

My point is parenting is a learning experience, and the first child to a certain extent is a guinea pig. I remember after we had some parenting conflict I apologized and said to Bill, "I am sorry, but there is no manual on parenting. You just have to learn by your mistakes as you go." I think it all worked out in the end. He made Eagle Scout, no small achievement. (My research reveals only 5 percent of scouts attain Eagle.) Bill is self-driven, graduated college, and is married with children. He has a great job and is a responsible, contributing, thriving member of society. Loves his family and the New York Giants football team. Moral of the story: firstborns can succeed despite the deficiencies of their green inexperienced first-time parents.

***

When Matt was seventeen and Andrew was five, the three of us went to Disney World. What a fun trip, and with a golf backstory which I will come back to. But I digress. Back to my food line of thought. The night before we departed, Matt was working late at the local convenience store where he was a stock boy and we had planned that he would sleep at our house since we had a very early start to the airport. He showed up at eleven o'clock with his food bag in hand—double-bacon cheeseburger, large fries, and a very large soda. Teenage boys actually eat like this. And as an emerging senior citizen, my stomach was doing flips as I looked upon the considerable stash of food and thought, *How in the world can he sleep after eating this?* But he got up bright and early the next morning and when I asked him if he slept okay, he said, "Oh, yeah!"

I mentioned above that there was a golf backstory to our All Guys Disney trip. So the backstory is that on some cold January day in New Jersey, one of my most beloved friends, business and golf mentor asked me if I could join him and some other business types for a four-day golf getaway in Florida. You know, he said, 80 degrees, golf all day, nap, food and adult beverage all night. I had never done anything so "irresponsible" in my life, up to now always having some work, life, or kids obligations. But I really wanted to go on this trip. Having spent many years in sales, the thought occurred—start selling! Or even better, start negotiating. Marriage is, after all, better as an equal negotiation versus a pressure-selling situation. Of course. *Just lay it out to your wife as a quid pro quo*, I thought to myself. I said to Cyndee,

"So ... here is the situation. I have a chance to go on a fabulous inexpensive four-day golf boondoggle in Florida with a bunch of guys, and I really want to make it happen. But I don't want you to feel like you are getting the short end of the stick, so think about it and come back to me and tell me what you want in return to make this feel like a totally even and fair transaction." She said, "Okay, let me think about it and I will get back to you." *Gosh, that was easy enough*, I thought!

The next morning she told me that she had thought it over and what she wanted in return was to go away herself for four days with her lady friends at some time later in the year. Faster than you can say deal, I said, "Deal!" I went to Florida and had the most wonderful and memorable experience and met some individuals who I am very good friends with many years later as a result of "bonding" on our golf trip.

***

Fast forward seven months later. We had booked a vacation for three—me, Cyndee, Andrew—to go to Disney World for a week. It was August and well, gosh, Cyndee was pregnant with Raquel! She was starting to feel uncomfortable and the thought of traveling to Disney, stuck in a hotel ... did I mention pregnant ... so she was thinking she did not want to go and would feel more comfortable in her home with her bed. All made sense to me.

Then she says, "Remember that deal we had where I get to go away by myself. I want to do a staycation here at home while you take (five-year-old) Andrew to Disney World for a week." My initial reaction was… "Hold on." The thought of chasing a high-energy five-year-old nonstop 24/7 by myself for a week in a gigantic park with 50,000 other people sounded like a really bad deal. I did not think I could fill the shoes of both Mom and Dad on vacation. Then she said, "Take Matt. You three go with my blessing." Matt was seventeen at the time, heading off to college soon. This would likely be the last time to go on vacation together.

Matt said yes and so he, Andrew, and I went to Disney World for a week and had one of the most fun and memorable experiences of my life. Sleep in. Stay up late. Experience the park all day and then jump in the pool. It might be 11:00 PM… "Dad, can we order cheeseburgers from room service?" Sure, go for it. 1:00 AM… "Oh, Dad, do I have to brush my teeth?" No, go to bed. 1:30 AM… "Oh, Dad, do I have to get into my pajamas?" No. Just go to sleep.

Okay, so dads are not moms and are known to slack and take shortcuts to get the job done. But we had the greatest time with both the guys bonding, all the rides… and for goodness' sake, it was Disney World! I have my wife to thank for this great idea and one of the most memorable experiences of my life. And a golf game was the impetus that started the chain reaction moving.

***

We were at back-to-school night when Andrew was in eighth grade, and we were told that each of the students wrote a letter to their parents located in the child's desk. Up to this point, I would have described Andrew as a cute little kid who loved insects, animals, and chasing butterflies with his little net. And with lots of lessons, practice and play, he had become very proficient at both golf and tennis. He almost hurt me with his serve on several occasions when I would guess wrong and jump into his blistering fast serve. So we opened the letter and were caught totally off guard by our thirteen-year-old's message that says in so many words,

Dear Mom and Dad,

I love you. Life is great. Family is great. You are great. Everything is great. But I do not want to play golf or tennis anymore. I want to play lacrosse and do wrestling.

Lacrosse? Whirling a rock projectile at unprotected bodies? Wrestling? Pulling arms out of sockets? Throwing bodies around? It just did not sound like Andrew. Looking back, there was pre-puberty Andrew and post-testosterone Andrew. Nothing really unusual here, just something I should have known, with him being the third son I raised. So he traded in his butterfly net for a wrestling singlet. He hit the weights, consumed whey protein in abundance, and turned into a muscular beast with an insatiable appetite.

Andrew reminded me of the Roman Empire, of which I read had this massive need to find and consume vast amounts of protein to fuel the needs of their warriors. It was the same with Andrew. A dozen eggs, pound of lean ground beef, and a couple shakes of whey protein was often a typical day for wrestling and lacrosse in the past and Olympic weightlifting in the present. Which brings me to the topic of pork loin and a question: who eats pork loin on a golf course in the middle of a round? Answer: Andrew.

Most people will get a hot dog at the halfway point or bring a sandwich. But one day as he and I were playing golf and sharing a cart heading to the second hole— second hole! —he was unwrapping this giant piece of aluminum foil. I asked, "What in the world do you have there?" To which he unveiled a massive piece of pork loin left over from the night before. (It was probably intended as a leftover dinner for four!) He said, "What? I was hungry!" I just shook my head, laughed, and moved on. Young boys and their appetites.

***

From the fairways, let me swing back to family ties for a moment. It is enough of a struggle and a statistical long shot that you will both love and like everyone in your immediate family. But once you start adding in the in-laws into the equation, well generally speaking you can throw all the probabilities out the window. My married children have all found great spouses with wonderful families. When there is a call to party together, we actually look forward to it and have a great time. How many people can say that? Thanks be to God! All glory and honor goes above! That is all I can say.

***

A golf course was the venue my future son-in-law John chose to ask me for my daughter Jackie's hand in marriage. We had never played before, but John set up a foursome with me, him, and two of my sons, Matt and Bill, with whom he had become good friends.

When Cyndee heard about the outing, she said to me, "He is going to ask you for your approval to marry Jackie."

"You really think so?" I said.

"Yes," she replied.

"I don't think so."

"What do you mean you don't think so?"

"I just don't think so."

Spoiler alert: always trust your wife's intuition.

The outing came together. John and I shared a golf cart for 18 holes and four and a half hours together. We had a lot of chit chat about work and golf but nothing about marriage. Afterwards, the four of us had burgers and beer, more talk about sports, work, and lots about the day of golf we just had. It was time to go. We all said our goodbyes and headed for the parking lot. I was thinking to myself, *Well, well, well, I guess Cyndee was wrong. No marriage proposal, blessing, approval ... whatever.* When we got to the parking lot, we all shook hands again and started heading in four directions. *No marriage discussion,* I mused to myself

Then I heard someone walking behind me, and John's voice saying, "Mr. Cordivari, I would like to talk to you about something important."

Two conversations immediately shot in my head. One: *Well, isn't this dandy.... This is quite the happy day.* And two: *Of course, my wife was right!*

With just the two of us standing in the middle of the parking lot, and even having been tipped off by my wife's intuition (or did she have inside information from Jackie?!), regardless, I said, "Sure, John. Why don't we go somewhere a little more conducive to talking?"

We found a little bench overlooking the entire course and there we had our chat. He told me of his intentions. I told him of my expectations of love and support of a husband marrying my daughter. And my approval was granted. Another major family event taking place near a fairway.

***

Our summers were spent at our mountain house in a golf course community in North Carolina. At this stage of life, it was me and Cyndee, Andrew and Raquel. The older children were getting married and starting their own lives. But life in the mountains was great family time and quality time. Swimming, rafting, hiking, dining, tennis, golf, and napping! We had it all going. I particularly loved my time playing golf and tennis when they were in their formative years. Every summer we played many rounds of golf together. *What a blessing*, I often thought, *to have your child as a captive audience for four hours on a golf course, in the sunshine, surrounded by God's majestic golf course landscaping and architecture.* Many rounds stand out but for various reasons, the following episode had great learning value for me and I hope Andrew.

***

It was a beautiful day. We had been to church, had lunch, and it was a very quiet and relaxed Sunday afternoon of golf unfolding. Many other residents had started back for work on Monday. It was as though the golf course belonged to just me and Andrew. I was psyched for a great day of golf and I wanted to lead by example and teach my son golf by having a great round and shooting a low score. He would see what great golf looked like, and would learn and do.

But alas, it was not to be. Every golfer can relate to what was about to unfold. By the third hole, it was clear to me that it was going to be "one of THOSE days." And by "those" I mean one of those days where nothing goes right, everything that can go wrong does go wrong, and just forget the scorecard because you will never dig yourself out of the hole you have dug in the early going. I was thinking that my son was looking at me and thinking, *Gosh, Dad, you stink.* He would never say that but he could very well be thinking it.

I was looking up to the heavens and invoking Psalm 22, "My God, My God, why have you forsaken me?" *Really, God. This is a debacle. This is not what I expected. Not what I prayed for. I thought I could count on you. My son thinks I am an awful golfer.* And on and on I went.

The still small voice inside said, *Bill, he knows your golf game. He has played with you many times. He knows you know how to play golf. He knows you know how to hit a golf ball. But today, my plan – not your plan – is I want you to teach him how you behave on a golf course when things are not going well. When things are going downright awful. He has seen some really bad role models on TV and even on your home course. Teach Andrew how a Cordivari man and a man after God's own heart behaves when things do not go well.*

Okay, Lord, that was not my plan but I hear THE PLAN loud and clear! So as I continued to struggle, instead of giving in to the urge to scream the obscene or even break a club in two over my knee ... I would chuckle or look at him and just shake my head with a slight smile and say with a touch of acceptance and resignation, "You know, Drew, some days it just doesn't work out in terms of scoring. And on this kind of days you have to remind yourself that it is a privilege and a blessing just to be out here on a golf course. It is a spectacular sunny day ... and hey, I get to spend four hours with Andrew Cordivari. What kind of awesome day is this?"

As I tallied my score of 100 or worse at the end of the round, the still voice said, *Well done, Bill. I am proud of you. That was an important lesson today.*

***

I was on a business trip in the late nineties and was calling home after dinner to check in with the family as was our ritual. I was chatting with Cyndee a bit and then she said, "Andrew (then four years old) wants to tell you something." I said, "Okay, put him on." I could hear him rustling the phone. "What's up, big guy?" I said to him. Without missing a beat, he says, "Dad, I want to be a big brother. I want us to have another baby so I can be a big brother to somebody."

This took me by total surprise and from here began another major facet of my faith walk. Another baby? I would be a father for the fifth time but I would be forty-eight maybe forty-nine years old when the baby was born. I did not even want to ponder the future math of how old for college, graduation, marriage. How much would college cost in twenty years. Where would I find the energy? That, I think, was my main concern...where would I find the energy? Work and family demands were draining. The jobs were getting bigger and so was the family.

I certainly wanted to honor my wife's desire and my young son's request that we have another baby, but I was really hung up on the passing of time, the calendar, and the energy factor kept creeping back.

> So Sarah laughed to herself thinking, "After I am worn out will I have a child, especially when my husband is too old?"
> - Genesis 18:12

Yes, I kept circling back to the singular thought... *Am I too old to be a father again?* It was weighing heavily on my mind and my spirit. Yes, the Evil One was probably having a good time with me. I was easy picking. Sow a little doubt here. Plant a devious question there. Stir... and keep him off balance. Keep him confused and looking in all of the wrong directions.

Where was my faith? Where was my trust in the Lord of the Impossible? In my small mind and weak faith, I did not think it humanly possible to be a father again.

Jesus looked at them and said, "With man this is impossible, but with God all things are possible."

- Matthew 19:26

Several weeks went by as we wrestled with this question. We sought out our pastor for advice. He said, "The question should not be… what does the husband want or what does the wife want. The question and the prayer should be… where is God leading this marriage?" I left that session thinking that I already knew the right answer but was blocking it. In the ensuing days, I prayed to the effect, "Lord, I know what the right decision is. But it does not feel right somewhere inside me. I am willing to trust you but will you help make it feel right?"

A few nights later I had a dream. There are many Bible stories where an Angel or the Lord or a Spirit appears or reveals something important in a dream. I had a dream that seemed so real. In the dream, I had just returned home from work and I came to the front door. As I stepped inside, this little baby girl with curly hair and wearing only a diaper came running over to me and yelled out, "Daddy!" as she playfully slapped me on the leg then turned around and ran away giggling wildly.

I woke up with tears in my eyes. I had tears of joy. I had tears of gratitude. I had tears of feeling God's love ever real. I had a big smile on my face. I had reached the end of this struggle in the spiritual wilderness and came out the other side. I wanted another baby. I was ready for another baby. I did not know how it was all supposed to work out or where the energy would come from, but I was trusting in my awesome God.

"Trust in the Lord with all your heart and lean not on your own understanding. In all of your ways acknowledge him and he will make your paths straight."

- Proverbs 3:5–6

Cyndee became pregnant and the pregnancy proceeded without any complications, praise the Lord. I do remember an amusing aspect, however.

In one of our doctor visits with Cyndee's awesome OBG, we were all having difficulty coming to an alignment of the facts around the date of conception. The doctor threw up his arms, laughed, and said, "What the heck. Let's not argue over the date. These things are all a miracle anyway!" Our baby was born on December 8. As I recalled from my Catholic education … December 8 is commemorated as the feast of the Immaculate Conception! Who says God does not have a sense of humor!

Our little baby was a girl and we named her Raquel Renee. We later saw a plaque in a store that read, "Raquel means Joy." And we totally agreed with that. Renee is French for "Born Again." What a great name. This little girl has been endless joy and allowed me to be born again... yet again! Born again of an even greater faith in an all-loving and all-faithful God. And she is an immense source of joy every single day. I give all glory, honor, and praise to a loving God.

God and Golf Moment

Trust The Swing

It is a core point of golf instruction that you need to trust the swing.

If you are a golfer, you have heard this but if you are like me, we still have a hard time doing this. The club is designed to work with the universal laws of physics to propel the ball to its intended destination.

But the typical golfer has many negative and fearful thoughts going through their head. As a result, they think they have to hold the club tightly or focus on multiple swing thoughts to guide the ball before swinging. But that does not usually work out too well. Getting to a relaxed state and trusting the club and the swing to work like they are intended usually has a much better outcome.

In life, we need to trust God.

Jesus said, *"I will never forget nor forsake you."* We can trust God in the big and little things in life. Say a prayer, trust the Creator of you and all things and fight the inner programming of trying to over-control or over-worry about situations.

Chapter 7

The Brotherhood of Believers ... and Golfers!

"For whoever does the will of my Father in heaven is my brother and sister and mother."
                                    - Matthew 12:50

W ho is my brother? (Part 1)

I have been blessed to be brought into this world in a family with four brothers and a sister. And I like being the senior member of this Cordivari clan. It is an honor and a privilege. There was a time when I unfairly lauded my senior status over them, particularly when I was left home in charge as the babysitter. "New sheriff in town. Things are going to be different with Mom and Dad not home." Yes, a power trip. What an idiot. My siblings would of course bust me to my parents when they returned home. You just knew they would. And my dad would look at me with those twinkling blue eyes and, without saying anything, communicate, "Come on. You are better than that."

I am glad my siblings have forgiven me for that short period of my life when I was on a power trip. We were all close growing up and we have remained close all of these many decades later. Italians can be a vengeful lot and, growing up, we saw how "stupid little things" blown out of proportion could cause massive family strife and even brother not talking to brother or sister. It was perplexing to watch and at times to be part of the collateral damage. We all vowed that we would not let that happen to us. I think we have "broken the chain."

And if there was one other thing that bound us together as we were growing up and maturing, it was not golf but basketball. We grew up in the shadows of Villanova, Pennsylvania, and all six of us attended Villanova University. We became basketball fanatics and loved the school, and there was no doubt where were we going when it was time for college.

By the time we graduated from college and took our places in the world, there was no more big brother-little brother. All six of us had been raised well and jumped into the job market with a sense of responsibility and a competitiveness to excel. Mom and Dad had prepared us very well indeed. Two brothers went into law enforcement, one a direct marketing entrepreneur, one an aerospace engineer and GM, and sister is a mathematical straight-A whiz who went into accounting and finance.

We all played a little bit of golf with each other in various permutations as we were finding our way in the world and with our careers. But in recent years, as our children were growing up and/or we have moved to positions of greater responsibility but also flexibility, we have been putting foursomes together more and more frequently.

***

But we do have a fairly recent golf story that involves most of us and is in our highlights film. The 2013 US Golf Open was held at the Merion Golf Club in the shadows of where we grew up. As kids, our hallowed grounds were the Villanova Field House for world-class college basketball, and the Merion Golf Club for golf. Any golfer knows that Merion is primo and always in the Top 10 US golf courses. The topography is spectacular, the course architecture magnificent (I am running out of superlatives!), and some of the mansions surrounding it would be worthy of the Great Gatsby era.

Anyway, Rich, Rob, and I got tickets to the US Open in 2013 and we were very excited to spend the day together watching most of the world's greatest golfers upfront and personal. We were all looking forward to the big day and, as golfers are apt to do, we were monitoring the weather hourly leading up to the big day. Unfortunately, the weather forecast did not look good and was deteriorating towards our game day.

On the big day, we met for breakfast at Dad's house, a couple of miles from the course. Parking was going to be a mess, so Dad offered to drive us which we accepted. As we left his house, it was drizzling. As we approached the course, it was raining hard. Just as we got out of the car, it was coming down sideways. (Are you kidding me? Oh, God, do not forget nor forsake me!)

We were following a long path and somewhat protected from the rain by a forest of tall trees. But we were the only ones heading in; everyone else was heading out to the various hospitality suites. "Play has been suspended!" someone shouted to us. They likely were thinking that we were clueless. But we were not clueless. We were resolved, resolute, persistent...crazy? We really did not have a backup plan beyond hang out at the course. We pressed on and now we were really in "no man's land." We were too far from the entrance, stuck in the middle of the course, and play had been suspended. Silent prayer for some miracle. Waiting...waiting...no response. Hmmm. Okay, not getting any divine intervention here.

The rain was persistent but now thunder and lightning were rolling in. We did our best to find "shelter" under tall trees. BOOM went the thunder. FLASH went the lightning nearby. Okay, so this was where I guess you would be looking to the senior brother for a plan or solution. "Not good," I said. Rich and Rob nodded to the obvious. BOOM...FLASH continued. "Well," I said, "if you have to go, this is a heck of a place. The Merion Golf Course in the middle of the US Open! You can't pick a better place." Rich and Rob laughed hard as they probably thought, *Bill is really a sicko when it comes to golf!*

Another BOOM-FLASH... whoa, back to reality. We spotted a tent not too far away. It was a giant hospitality tent sponsored by the United States Golf Association (USGA). And to get into these tents, you prepay on top of your ticket. "Let's make a run for the tent," which we did. There was an overhang that we huddled under as the monsoon continued. Getting wet was secondary at this point. Stuck outdoors in a lightning storm with no backup plan was the priority issue. It was past funny at this point. As we huddled, I said, "What do you think...5...7 minutes max before some USGA official comes out and tells us to move along since we did not buy tickets. "Yes" was the consensus. About 5 minutes had passed when the door up at the top of the ramp opened and a woman came running towards us in the rain. "Here we go," I mumbled. "Yep, that didn't take long. She is going to tell us to scram," said a brother.

"Men, men... get out of the rain!," she said. "It's not safe out here. Come inside. Come on inside." And as we entered this gigantic, endless, oversized hospitality suite, she beckoned us, "Have some coffee. Get some food –omelettes on the left. Here is the Wi-Fi code, sit down and enjoy."

Well! I didn't see that coming. We were in there about two–three hours just chilling. Giant flat screens everywhere and everybody nice as could be. We were having such a good time eating, drinking ("Bar is open"), kibitzing, telling stories… that we did not notice the sun had come out. "Play resumes in 30 minutes," someone announced. Gosh, let's get ready for some golf!

The rest of the day was hot, sunny, humid—in my calculus… perfect for golf. Our clothes dried out from the rain and now got wet again from the sweat. We were out on the course for six hours, saw great golf, enjoyed the surroundings… and we lived happily ever after. What a perfect day. Spending time with the people you love watching the game that you love in a place that you love.

***

I often say that in my experience, God answers all prayers. It is just that he answers them in his time and way. And perhaps he doesn't give you what you want, but instead he gives you what you need. Or he doesn't give you what you asked for… he gives you twice what you asked for. Sometimes he appears not to answer your prayers, but I have learned to trust that He probably has something else going on that is what He thinks you really need, so stay tuned.

Anyway, on this particular day, when things were looking bleak hiding under the tall trees from the lightning, and I was lacking in faith ... it all turned out even better than any of us expected. And a special note of thanks to that "angelic" woman who brought us inside and truly treated us with "hospitality" in the hospitality tent! Hebrews 13:2 comes to mind...

"Do not forget to show hospitality to strangers, for by so doing some people have shown hospitality to angels without knowing it."

In this case, I am suggesting that she was the angel and we were the strangers badly in need of hospitality!

***

"Who is my brother?" (Part 2)

Gregg Mayo is my brother-in-law on my wife's side of the family. They say that you can pick your spouse but you can't pick the family that goes with it. In my case I won the lottery. My wife is more than I deserve. Her parents are the nicest and most decent people you will ever meet. And the extended family represents the best of Southern culture. This includes Cyndee's sister Helen and her husband Gregg who would become a great friend, a confidant on business, politics, life, and someone as insane about golf as I am. For many, many years he was my invited partner to a four-day member guest golf tournament hosted by the club where I had membership. They were some of the funnest days I can recall. We had the whole faith, family, and fairways mojo going at the annual Member-Guest tournament all of those years. I will always treasure the special times together.

***

My first exposure to Gregg took place during our trips to his home in Birmingham, Alabama, to visit him and Helen when our kids were young. Gregg's kids were also young, and seemed like they lived on the baseball diamond. Gregg was always in some coaching capacity or helping out. One of his hallmarks is his voice.

When I was in the military and attending Officer Candidate School, they would speak of a "command voice." They meant a loud, firm voice that would command respect. With this in mind, I want to tell you that Gregg has a command voice! It rises above the crowd. And I don't mean he is bossy or noisy, I mean only that he has a solid voice. He can make animals stop in their tracks. More about that in a moment.

***

One time we were playing golf together in Birmingham and the course was favored by some large black birds … crows, if I had to guess. They kept landing on our golf cart and sniffing around

for food whenever we walked away from the
cart. I had taken my expensive watch off and put
it in a plastic sandwich bag to keep it clean and
protected, placing the plastic bag in the storage
compartment on top of the cart. We were putting
on the green when a crow came along, saw the
plastic bag with something bright and shiny
inside...and concluded...food! The crow took
off with the plastic bag in its mouth, and started
flapping its wings, looking like some jumbo jet
slowly getting airborne. I was having a bird (that
is what you say, right?) and I was running after the
dang thing, yelling, "Yo...Yo, bird...bird!" And
behind me I heard Gregg's booming voice shout,
"YO, BIRD!" And to my relief the bird dropped the
bag with my watch and I think it had a bathroom
moment as well. Thank you, Gregg, and for your
command voice I still have that watch.

***

Not only does Gregg have a command voice, but
he also has what to my Yankee ears sound like
a thick, deep, Southern drawl. One day we were
playing and he was in the sand bunker on the other
side of the green as the "cart girl" drove up to my
side of the green. (I have never seen a cart guy —
you think they think females can sell more food
than guys?) Anyway, I yelled out to him, "Do you
need anything?" And he yelled across the green to
me, "I need a sanwidge." I asked the cart girl what

kind of sandwiches she has, then I went over to Gregg and said, "She has ham, turkey or tuna." He smiled and said, "No, not a sandwich…I need a sand wedge! Boy, you must be from New Jersey!"

***

One time we had gone to Birmingham to spend the Thanksgiving holiday with Gregg, Helen, and the extended family. And traditionally, the BIG college football game and rival grudge match between Auburn and Alabama takes place that weekend. Such was the case during this visit. Backstory: Gregg is 101 percent all-Auburn. Went to Auburn, bleeds blue and orange…gives the secret code around Birmingham which is "War Eagle." If you went to Alabama, your special passcode is "Roll Tide." We were in solid War Eagle territory and Gregg was pacing and nervous starting around breakfast. He looked at me and my son Andrew and said, "Beeel (Bill), An-DREW…are you guys ready for the big game tonight? We are going to watch it here so we are getting set." And then he says, "It is a tradition around here that on Auburn-Alabama day, we tape our ankles and put our eye black on for the game." (I really thought he meant it.) After a pause with likely a dazed look on my face, I say, "Are you serious?" Big booming laugh, "NO! I am just having some fun with y'all." But we won't be sitting for the game.

Well, he was telling the truth on that part. For three hours he paced the family room, cheered, booed, called the plays before they were called. He stood, paced some more, shouted, screamed … and thank goodness Auburn won on this night. Later at bedtime, I asked Andrew what he thought of the game. He shook his head and said, "Wow, Uncle Gregg is really intense." Ha-ha. Perfect. It was better than going to the stadium. We had a one-man crowd to guide and entertain us.

***

Gregg and I played six or seven years in a row as partners in the annual member-guest tournament at my club, Mountain Air Country Club. We played good golf, great golf, and awful golf at various times — because that is how golf is. But we always had a great time. Gregg just has a way with people and on top of being a Southern gentleman with a sense of Southern hospitality and as I previously mentioned what I call a drawl, he fit right in with most of the club members who hailed from first homes south of the Mason-Dixon line. I think he knew more people than I did … and I was the member, he was the guest. He just has a natural inclination to engage people as humans first and meet them wherever they may be in life. We might pass the guy fixing an irrigation problem on the course and Gregg would chat him up, "What's going on? Looks like ya got a mess on your hands.

You doin' good?" And a natural conversation would ensue. As I said, he has a way with people. I wish I could be more like that.

***

The Member-Guest tournaments were big deals in that there were over sixty participants, official money and "unofficial" money involved, a leaderboard posted daily to see where things stood and, if you were playing poorly, for the whole world to see! The atmosphere was one of "friendly competition." Depending upon who you were playing, it could be strictly friendly or strictly competitive in tonality. I think Gregg and I strove to find the right balance. There was always a fabulous spread of food and beverage as part of the four-day event, so some people just showed up to have a good time. We were in the second category. Gregg would say, "I didn't drive six hours to eat." And I would wink and say, "No, we are IN IT TO WIN IT!" And we would both laugh and high-five. So we were very competitive but we learned over the years watching ourselves and our competitors as to how to strike the right balance between playing hard versus not being a jerk. I like to think we got it right.

***

Gregg brought out the best in me as a golfer, as a competitor, and as a man in faith. We wanted to play hard but not send the wrong message. Over the years, we got into this nice little ritual before setting out for a day of golf. We would have the car all packed up. Check, check, check … that we had sunscreen, chewing tobacco (Gregg), snacks, enough balls (!), etc. And then before we would pull out of the driveway, we would take our hats off, bow our heads, and say a prayer that went something like this:

> *"Dear Lord, thank you for this awesome day. We thank you for the honor and privilege and the blessing of being able and healthy enough to play golf. We thank you for the beauty of your creation all around us. For just being here and our time together. Lord, we pray that we would play great golf today. That we would play our best … and that you would throw a couple lucky breaks our way as well. We want to win today, but first and foremost we want to conduct ourselves as Christian gentlemen in all that we say and do, that we will bring glory to the kingdom. And we pray all of this in Jesus' name. Amen!"*

And then one of us would say, "Let's go get 'em!" Me, Gregg, Mountain Air, and the annual Member-Guest is for me the essence of faith, family, and fairways all coming together. Thanks be to God!

***

Who is my brother? (Part 3) When Cyndee and I married and settled in Bedminster, New Jersey, we found a solid church. That led me to a good men's group which led me to an early morning Bible study held every Friday at a local restaurant and bar.

The founder of this Bible study was a local restaurant entrepreneur by the name of Jack Welch. Jack had attended Cornell and majored in hospitality. He and his roommate wrote a business plan to start a restaurant business and they executed that plan after graduation. Year by year Jack started or ran more than twenty different restaurants which had great names like Willie's Taverne, The Thirsty Turtle, The Famished Frog, The Bamboo Grill, and so many more. But along the way, Jack's faith caught fire and he came up with the Big Idea to convene Bible studies in his restaurants on different days of the week. Each started at 6:30 AM so those working could still leave by 7:30 AM and get to work at a respectable time.

I came to know Jack Welch very well over the years and highly respected him. We went to the same Bible study on Fridays, we attended the same church and saw each other on Sundays, and we hung in the same golf circles. In terms of golf, Jack was about the same as me — an average player but very competitive. (More on that in a moment.)

Jack and I roomed together for a week on a mission trip to Honduras where we stayed in a spartan hotel. We were both on the "rooming snoring" list. It was like a contest each night on who could snore the loudest. I think Jack won! Whether or not it was serving the needy in Honduras or the overfed in New Jersey, Jack had a heart for hospitality. I told him that I thought this made his career in restaurant and hospitality more of a calling than a job. He said, "I think you are right."

***

In 2013, Jack and a bunch of the guys from the Friday morning Bible study went on a four-day golf/spiritual retreat to the house of our mutual friend, Jack Frost in Duck, North Carolina. We had about a dozen guys staying in two houses. We took turns making breakfast and dinner. We had morning devotional and evening Bible studies around themes. And we golfed all day. Perfect! I led the after-dinner devotional and discussion one evening. (More about that in a moment.)

I mentioned that Jack and I traveled in the same golf circles — so we knew each other's ways around a golf course — and while close friends and brothers in Christ, we were very competitive on the golf course. I mean to the point of challenging each other's scores on a particular hole now and again and other such adult "nonsense." Golf can bring out the little kid in mature men.

So one day as we were finishing lunch and getting ready for the afternoon round, our host was coming around distributing the scorecards for the afternoon's matches and he gave our group card to me. (Jack was in my group.) Jack said, "I will take the card." I said, "No, he gave the card to me." And this went back and forth. I said, "What's the big deal? He gave me the card?"

We both knew what the big deal was. Who has the card records the score. There may be a point of confusion or ambiguity in scorekeeping, etc., particularly in a "friendly game" where the strict attention to rules can be flexible or open to negotiation. Neither one of us gave any ground and we both headed off for the afternoon in a little bit of a huff with each other. I think I was actually brooding over it—yes, I can be a complete idiot at times. We did not really talk about it again that day and I did not have the opportunity to speak with him before I left for home the next morning. This was in May of 2013.

***

I did run into Jack the next week back in New Jersey at Friday Bible study. He saw me across the room, waved me towards him, and pulled me off to the side. He said, "You got a minute? There is something I need to tell you." (And I was thinking, *No – we are not going to discuss the scorecard tiff, are we? No*, we were not.) He said, "I just want to tell you that the Bible Study and the discussion you led on the last night was the highlight of my trip. It really hit home. I am so grateful and I have decided that will be my spiritual focus going forward the rest of the year." (My talk was about setting aside some of your best time and not just left over time to connect with God each day and preferably in the morning.) He continued, "Hey, Billy, say Hi to Cyndee. And how are the kids doing? How is Andrew doing in college?"

I felt small but glad that Jack was one of the major people in my orbit and had been so pivotal supporting my faith walk for a long time. That was the last conversation we had. A couple of weeks later, Jack dropped dead on the golf course making the turn between the 9th and 10th holes. He was playing with his Bible study buddies. It was such a sad day. My friend Andy Stewart who had been playing with Jack texted me late that evening. His short text said it all: "We lost a GREAT man today."

***

I learned a lot of lessons from Jack Welch over the years, but I particularly learned some critical things over the last two months that he was with us:

- Don't be so thin-skinned. Keep your eyes on the prize.
- Serve other people with a big heart for hospitality.
- No timeline is promised to anyone. Seize the day. A cliché perhaps, but so true.

- If you love someone, if they are important to you, for goodness' sake let them know! Jesus said, *"You know not the hour or the day."*

***

In addition to Jack Welch, I have also met and befriended many other men from church and local Bible study, and they have all made significant contributions to my faith walk and shaped where I am in the journey this day. I have also made solid kinships on the golf course with them which I find most interesting.

- Ron Peri was my first Adult Education Sunday School teacher when I returned from the spiritual wilderness and got back into a church. He helped me understand the teachings of the Bible and ignited a desire to know more and to pursue on my own. Ron has great credibility with the guys. He went to seminary where he got steeped in the Bible but felt called to the marketplace, not the pulpit. He joined IBM as a computer consultant and later started his own highly successful entrepreneurial aerospace industry software company. He has spread the "good news" of the gospel to thousands by his actions in everyday workplace interactions.

- Jack Frost is a longtime friend who over twenty-five years ago strongly suggested that I come to the Friday Bible study and I am very glad that I succumbed to his urging! We have enjoyed many a round of golf at his home course at his beloved alma mater Rutgers, and we both have a mutual love of North Carolina golf.
- Andy Stewart, a colleague of mine from Johnson and Johnson — has become known as my "partner in crime" as we developed this natural calling to teach Bible study together as a duet. We are alike in many dimensions and unlike in many other that we complement each other well. This experience has made teaching fun and made me bold to volunteer "us!" for whenever there is an opening or a need. More about golf below.
- Barry Abell retired from selling bonds on Wall Street and went into full-time Men's Ministry initially focused on business executives but now out in the New Jersey suburbs where the audience is any men who want to join us at 6:30 AM on Friday mornings. He has been our lead teacher for over twenty years and we have learned much from him.
- Dan Bove steps in often to lead when Barry is traveling on behalf of the gospel or serving his family. Dan was very successful

as a marketing executive in the technology field and when he hit his midlife career crisis, he felt the nudge of the Holy Spirit into full-time ministry helping the addicted with a nonprofit organization called Pause which he founded. Dan is thriving in his new pursuit and has less time for golf ... and I do not think he cares!

- Jim Johnston is a BIG thinker and doer. After Jack Welch passed and his businesses were sold, it looked like our long-standing Bible study was becoming homeless with no adequate venue to meet. Jim, who is a devoted follower of Christ, a successful insurance entrepreneur extraordinaire, and a longtime member of the group, stepped up and made his company cafeteria available to us. It has been our cozy new setting for the last few years. Jim also hosts a community-wide Nativity lighting and Christmas caroling event on the front lawn of his company each year. His life reflects a wonderful and unabashed witness of our great faith.

- Tom Ferguson also greatly helped my golf game, but more importantly he showed me how to be bold with my faith. Tom founded and built up a very successful advertising agency bearing his name. After he sold the company, he threw himself into philanthropy and raising money for many Christian and other charitable organizations. He is the consummate gentleman, devoted family man, avid golfer, and most impressively walks the walk when it comes to our faith. He has been a personal trailblazer for me and a role model. He saw me tipping a caddie one day, pulled me aside and said, "Oh, come on, Mr. Big Shot Johnson & Johnson executive. Don't be so cheap! Spread the money around to all the hard workers and less fortunate." I never forgot that "golf" lesson.

- Phil Gillespie is a close friend, a devoted family man, a man with a strong Christian faith and in terms of golf...a fanatic like me. Sometimes I think he is even more possessed by the game than me. And that is saying a lot. Which helps explain why I love to hang around with him. A few years ago, I convened a Saturday morning foursome of me and Phil, introduced him to my great friend Andy Stewart from church and former Johnson and Johnson days, and a close friend, Bob Kessler.

- I have only known Bob Kessler for the last few years through work, but having quickly become very good friends, we feel like we have been in each other's lives a long time. We are so similar in beliefs and values that people at work took to calling us BillBob! And one of the values Bob and I share is golf. Another value is faith. I respect Bob's Jewish faith and he respects my Christian faith. I don't work with Bob anymore and we miss our daily interactions. I recently saw him at the office Christmas party to which I had received a special invite. As we were parting, we gave each other a hug—a manly hug!—and he said, "Miss you, man. You are like my brother from another mother. Have a wonderful Christmas." I cannot tell you how much that meant to me. Bob does not usually share his soft side!

- Bob is a golfing maniac. Andy is a golf savant. Phil is a golf fanatic. My Saturday morning foursome included passionate golfing savants, maniacs, and fanatics. Oh, joy!

My youngest child, daughter Raquel, is not a golf devotee but she is aware of every nuance of what is going on in her daddy's world. She said, "Dad, you are so lucky that you get to play golf with your three best friends from church and work and the neighborhood. And you all get along so great." She is absolutely correct and I count it in my blessings.

All of the guys I mentioned above are my brothers in faith. And they all happen to be fun to golf with! But more importantly, they are all part of my personal "cloud of witnesses."

"Therefore since we are surrounded by such a great cloud of witnesses, let us throw off everything that hinders and the sin that so easily entangles and let us run with perseverance the race marked out for us."

- Hebrews 12:1

God and Golf Moment

Rip Up the Scorecard

One of the painful things about golf is the darn scorecard.

You must record every shot. Yes, *you must record every shot.* As the game is 18 holes in duration, if you have some really bad early holes, it is mentally painful to carry those sevens or eights (or worse) through the rest of the round. You start thinking, *I wish I could just rip up the scorecard and start over.* Unfortunately, you cannot.

But in life, it's amazing—we can rip up the scorecard. Whether young or old, whatever age or stage of life, even if we have a long and painful string of regrets, we can rip up the scorecard.

If we repent of our sinful choices, if we turn our lives over to Jesus and accept him as personal Lord and Savior… we are in effect ripping up the scorecard. Oh, yeah!

> *"For God did not send his Son Jesus into the world to condemn the world but to save the world through him."*
>   - John 3:17

Chapter 8

CALLED TO THE MOUNTAINS
❦

" The heavens declare the glory of God, the skies proclaim the work of his hands."

- Psalm 19:1

Growing up in the Philadelphia suburbs meant that summers included trips to the Jersey shore. My first venue was Ventnor just south of Atlantic City where my grandfather had a bay front house. In college, I had a house with a group of friends in Ocean City. As I married and had children, we migrated further south to Avalon and Stone Harbor. My personal recommendation is Stone Harbor, which I believe has one of the most beautiful long, wide, and white beaches you will find anywhere. And it is a cute little upscale family town as well. For the longest time, I was an ocean person. I loved the sand, the surf, the breeze, the squawk of the sea gulls. The sound of the ocean's waves lapping the shore at night is a great background sound for a tranquil sleep. There is and was much that I love about the beach and the ocean.

But something started to stir inside of me about mountains. Unconsciously, I started buying artwork of mountains and hung them in my office. One day in the late nineties, I told Cyndee that I was having visions of mountains.

"Visions of mountains?" she clarified.

"Yes, visions of mountains. I think we should find a house in the mountains."

She said, "Well, okay, I am on it,"

We had a trip here and there to mountain venues in upstate Pennsylvania and Vermont, but there were no sparks flying. Then one day there was a full page ad in the back of the *Wall Street Journal* with an aerial view of a place called Mountain Air in Burnsville, North Carolina. Looking at the aerial shot of a lush golf course in the midst of the Blue Ridge Mountains, my impression was... *Well, this is interesting*. Like Augusta National Golf Course meets the *Sound of Music*. I expected to see Julie Andrews dancing across the green spinning and singing. My next impression was that this had to be slick advertising and enhanced photography. It could not possibly look this good in reality.

I asked Cyndee what she thought and she said that she knew Burnsville because she had babysat there for her cousins when she was growing up. She was born in Albemarle, North Carolina, and had relatives sprinkled in both North and South

Carolina. She said we need to check it out—which we did. And it was love at first sight.

We purchased a home overlooking the 18th green and with a long view of the mountains at which I never tire of looking. Some days there are five, six, maybe ten rows of mountain ranges of beautiful green pines. The sky is either sunny and blue or grey with powerful clouds blowing through. The sunrises and sunsets are majestic. No other word does justice to the setting.

So what does any of this have to do with faith, family, and fairways? Well, the fairway part is obvious. It is called Mountain Air Country Club because it features a world-class eighteen-hole golf course with beautiful landscaping and architecture sculpted into the Blue Ridge Mountains. There are about 400-plus homes, town houses, condos and villas, but when you are in the valley or driving through downtown, you hardly see a home. Everything is tastefully constructed to keep a natural feel to it.

The family part is that our home has been a great venue where our children spent many a summer growing up. It gave all of us a chance to chill and regroup from our "normal" hustle and bustle lives in New Jersey and in the frenetic culture of greater New York. Also, Cyndee's parents and family were not far away—so it gave her a chance to see them in the summer. We would have friends from all over come and visit now and then. My brothers and I got into a ritual of the Cordivari

Brothers October Golf Getaway at Mountain Air. Similarly, Cyndee would convene retreats with her family and friends at different times of the year. Mountain Air is where our family bonds, where we go to get recharged, and where we just soak up the peace and the beauty of God's awesome creation all around us.

Which brings me to the faith part. What does a golf course and the mountains have to do with faith? The primary answer is locale. Burnsville, North Carolina, is in the heart of the Southern Bible belt. The town center has a library, a bank, a restaurant, and four churches. That will give you some idea. The local people are the nicest I have met anywhere. They have a genuine decency and grounded approach to life best described as faith and family. People share their faith openly and without hesitating in the mountain towns of North Carolina. Up North, everyone is so uptight with political correctness ("Happy Holidays") that it is difficult to be yourself if you are a believer. You find yourself making a calculation—is this person safe to be myself with ... or will they take offense? And while I know we are called to be bold in the profession and beliefs of our faith, there is the reality of the impact and influence upon us in the culture in which we reside. Up North is one way of living, mainly secular and materialistic with a safe sprinkling of faith. Down South, the Christian faith is embedded in the culture. People expect that you go to church, read the Bible, and openly share discussions about your faith with one another. That is another great aspect of the time spent at Mountain Air. I feel like I rejuvenate my soul when I am there. We read that Jesus went to the mountains to pray and be close to God.

> *"In those days, Jesus went out to the mountain to pray, and He spent the night in prayer to God."*
> *- Luke 6:12*

My spirit is energized. My family is nearby. I can smell the fresh grass clippings of the 18th hole nearby. And I am nestled at a point 5,000 feet closer to Heaven. It all comes together at Mountain Air!

God and Golf Moment

The Beauty of Creation Is All Around Us

"O Lord Our Lord how majestic is your name in all of the earth. When I consider your heavens, the work of your fingers, the moon and the stars, which you have set in place, what is man that you are mindful of him?"
- Psalm 8:1–4

"The heavens declare the glory of God, the skies proclaim the work of his hands. Day after day, they pour forth speech; night after night, they display knowledge. There is no speech or language where their voice is not heard. Their voice goes out into all the earth, their words to the ends of the world."
- Psalm 19:1–4

The beauty and wonders of creation and a loving Creator are all around us.

I strongly believe this is never more so than when experiencing a perfectly manicured golf course with a fairway like a green carpet on a perfect blue sky day with just a right dash of the warm sun and of course, the splendor of mountains in the background.

Oh, joy! Oh, majesty! What a blessed soul I am. What blessed souls we are.

Chapter 9

A NATURAL LOVE OF GOLF
❧

"I tell ya, country clubs and cemeteries, the biggest wasters of prime real estate.."
- Rodney Dangerfield

With all due respect to one of the funniest lines about golf ever from Rodney Dangerfield as Big Al Czervik in the classic comedy *Caddyshack*, I can think of few better uses of real estate than churches ... and yes, golf courses! Which leads me to explain a passion for golf and a love of the game.

The flight of the ball. I grew up playing with wiffle balls, tennis balls, softballs, baseballs, footballs, and basketballs. Golf was the last game I took up. The male species is consumed with balls, everybody knows that. I will leave it to the shrinks to tell us why. But what I will tell you is that of all the balls utilized in the various games, none is more beautiful or captivating than the flight of a well-struck golf ball. I am talking about a shot where the metal club pinches the ball and the ground and the surlyn-encased ball explodes on an accelerating flight with a slight right to left "pro-draw" starting low, then rising and falling to earth where it was intended. It does not happen that often for me but when it does, it is mystical and addictive. It may not happen again for who knows how many shots, but you know it is possible and you know you are capable.

Being outdoors. I spend the majority of my life in a house, car, hotel or airplane breathing recirculated dusty air. I will go for a walk outside a couple times a week if schedule and weather permit. But I am usually watching the clock and have the next commitment to get to. Golf provides four hours outside taking in fresh air and feeling the warmth of the sun or the wind blow and that in itself is invigorating.

Golf course architecture, beauty, and challenge. There are few patches of ground more beautiful than a well-cared-for golf course. The early morning dew on the greens, the meticulous cut of the fairways, the smell of cut grass in the roughs, the hues of white and brown in the sand bunkers. Ponds and creeks are penalties if you land in them, but they provide added natural attractions to the well-crafted golf course.

Friends, family, and fairways coincide. I was reflecting about with whom it is that I play golf. The list includes my father, brothers, sister, five children, sons-in-law, brothers-in-law, most of my bosses present and former, and virtually all of my best friends. So not only do I love golf on its own, but I am usually sharing the experience with my favorite people on earth. The only one missing from the list is my wife and now that the children are growing up, she is saying that her time is coming. I look forward to welcoming her to the golf team!

The personal challenge. As a child, I started with baseball and football taught to me by my father. Our family moved as I was entering high school, and basketball was "the game" in my new neighborhood so I shifted to that. In college, I met some friends who introduced me to tennis, and that became my priority for many years. It was not until I was out of college that my brother Rob introduced me to golf. I quickly became hooked on the game even though my shots went all over the course and I produced almost every bad shot known to golf: hooks, slices, shanks, chunks, "chili-dips." Gosh, this game turned out to be the hardest of any I ever attempted. How can it be so hard to move a club from Point A to Point B and back to Point A while accomplishing a square clubface at impact to propel the ball on a straight line to its intended path? In my humble opinion, it is very hard to do! Many years later, I am still in the same struggle. There has been much progress and satisfaction along the way, but I am still a long way from "mission accomplished." I think most avid golfers would agree that with golf you never attain "mission accomplished!"

Competitiveness. Some people love to compete at anything and I am one. But as you get older and more mature, there are fewer outlets for competition. Some options go away because of aging—like tackle football. Some drift away due to maturity—like beer-chugging contests or keeping up with the Joneses and buying that new car you really don't like or need but you do to stay competitive. Maturity helps here. So that leaves mainly golf and doubles tennis as prime outlets for competition if you want to keep your knees surgery-free. But it is not by default alone that I find golf such a competitive game. Multiple forces come together to make it one of the most competitive experiences there is. You are competing against yourself, your fellow players, and the unique physical challenges of the golf course and the variable weather all at the same time.

The Equipment and Attire. Few sports or games require or offer as much equipment and attire options as golf. The list includes beautiful, colorful, genuine all-leather golf bags and large, shiny oversized titanium drivers. There are the solid flashy irons with plush grips and fashionable shoes with spikes that make a unique sound when walking across a floor or gravel path. Add to the array ball markers, tees, gloves, towels, divot-repair tools, caps, shirts, slacks, socks, sweaters, sweater-vests and rain gear. There are endless options for treating yourself to something new or making a personal statement about you and your relationship to golf. There are multiple ways you can release your inner child with fun golf purchases in any Pro Shop, golf retail outlet, or online.

Relaxation. I have been blessed with good jobs since I graduated college. I have also been showered with a loving wife, five children, and a large extended family. But work and family demands, aging loved ones, and an uncertain global environment makes for inevitable stress. Sleeping through the night is a rarity, but I think I am probably "normal" in this regard. But stress is bad and stress left unattended is very bad for the human system. I find nothing more relaxing than escaping outdoors with people I like playing a game I love. And I particularly like golf courses that forbid the use of cell phones while on the course. That gives you a legitimate excuse to prevent anything from interfering with living in the golf moment!

The Nineteenth Hole. Usually my golfing experiences are in warm or hot weather. As you walk off the 18th green shaking hands and all smiles with your comrades, drenched in sweat, speckled with sand, and a little mud here and there, nothing is as refreshing as a cold beer in the air-conditioned grill, a little finger food, and a retelling of the day's adventures. It is ritualistic and most guys expect it as an extension of the day. It is a great disappointment when someone says, "Sorry, I've got to run," because what they are really telling us is that there is a real world waiting for us to reenter ... soon.

Mountain Air Country Club. We own a home at Mountain Air Country Club located in Burnsville, North Carolina, at an elevation of 4900 feet. The club features a first-class well-manicured 18-hole golf course with elevated tees and greens surrounded by inspiring views of the Blue Ridge Mountains. The temperature during the summer is usually 74 degrees, the humidity is mild or nonexistent, and it rains most days for about an hour. I call it Heaven's climate control. Not only does it feel wonderful but it also contributes to the lush conditions of the golf course. Most of my golf at Mountain Air is with friends or family, but frequently it is just playing alone and enjoying solitude and outdoor beauty. I always stop and take in the panorama of the mountain views regardless of how my game is going. The staff and members at Mountain Air are exceptionally friendly. When the round is over, the day is not complete until a stop at Orville and Wilbur's (O and W's), an open-air bar and grill sitting at the top of the mountain and looking out on inspiring beauty. Hands down, O and W's is my favorite nineteenth hole anywhere!

So, is it any surprise why I love the game of golf?

God and Golf Moment

Keep It in the Fairway

Golf can be a brutal game. If you keep it in the middle of the fairway, where the grass is cut short, tight and lush, and where hazards are nowhere to be found, golf can be an easy and fun game.

There are many similarities in life. If you behave in a disciplined way and make good decisions and pray continuously for God's blessing and direction, life can offer much joy. There are no guarantees but much better odds for sure.

Golf and life can be painful and full of regrets when you stray from the fairway and end up in the rough or in painful situations. Too often, where we end up is impacted by poor choices, inadequate training, or a breakdown in personal discipline.

Fairways are narrow and good. Roughs are wide and bad.

Jesus had a point of view on this. *"Enter through the narrow gate. For wide is the gate and broad is the road that leads to destruction and many enter through it."* (Matthew 7:13)

Keep it in the fairway. Life does not need to be made more difficult than it is.

Chapter 10

THE GREATEST STORY EVER TOLD
〜

"All scripture is God-breathed and is useful for teaching, rebuking, correcting and training in righteousness so that the man of God may be thoroughly equipped for every good work."
— 2 Timothy 3:16–17

I love the Bible and I love my Christian faith. It has been a long journey with the expected mountains and valleys, several years in the spiritual wilderness, stumbling and falling. But with time, grace and loving people, I found my way. And I hope and pray that you will, too, if you are still wandering and seeking.

My faith gives life purpose, meaning, direction, explanation, finality. The opposite I imagine is seeing life as a vessel for optimum pleasure, self-centeredness, all pain avoidance, living in the moment only, no meaning and plenty of contradictions. Do we yearn for eternity? Of course. Is faith a necessary contrivance? I don't think so.

The Bible is the main vessel that has impacted my faith walk. Below is a snippet of verses that are sealed in my being. I like that phrase, "sealed in my being." What I mean by that is I have been hanging around with these verses for so long that they are a part of me, shaping and defining who I am, what I believe, and how I live. These are the pillars of my personal Bible knowledge that shape much of the joy and gratitude I seek to live out each day. Let me share some and elaborate their sweet meaning to me.

***

> *"Who told you that you were naked?"*
> - Genesis 3:11

The very first pages of the Bible in Genesis unpack a lot of the explanations of life. Whether you accept or debate it as a literal happening or an allegorical teaching episode, the messages are the *truth*. An all-loving, all-perfect God created humanity and gave them an abundance of free gifts with one restriction. *"You must not eat from the tree of the knowledge of good and evil."* They were only given one restriction. But the man and the woman, tempted by the serpent/evil one, chose to disobey God and the rest is history. They were ungrateful. They were greedy. They were lacking in trust.

When I was new in my faith, I thought this was the most unfair thing I had ever heard. All of humanity receiving capital punishment because of the sin of one man and his wife? But as my faith grew, I saw the regrettable fairness of it. We relive this scene almost every day with our ingratitude, greed, and lack of trust. This all bears witness to the truth of it. Before the fall, God said, "It is good." After the fall, we became naked to our sin.

But the apostle Paul tells us to consider that while we are under the curse of sin due to one man, Adam, so we are liberated by the death of one man, of the sacrificial lamb in Jesus Christ. The birth, life, death and resurrection of Jesus makes all fair.

***

"Am I my brother's keeper?"

\- Genesis 4:9

Of course we are our brother's keeper. We are each other's keeper. The things that can divide us are numerous. The pulls to seek division are an easy escape route. But Jesus instructs us to "love one another as I have loved you." When Jesus tries to get our attention, we should pay attention! We spread the love and the message of Jesus when we act to be our brother's keeper as well as the keeper of our sister, neighbor, stranger, and even enemy.

***

"For nothing is impossible with God. I am the Lord's servant, Mary answered. May it be to me as you have said. Then the angel left her."
- Luke 1:38

"An angel of the Lord appeared to Joseph in a dream and said, Joseph, son of David, do not be afraid to take Mary home as your wife because what is conceived in her is from the Holy Spirit. She will give birth to a Son and you are to give him the name Jesus because he will save his people from their sins. All of this took place to fulfill what the Lord had said through the prophet, The virgin will give birth to a son and they will call him Immanuel which means, God with us. When Joseph woke up, he did what the angel had commanded him and took Mary as his wife. But he had no union with her until she gave birth to a son. And he gave him the name Jesus."
- Matthew 1:20–25

The strong faith and witness of the young girl who would play a pivotal role shaping history is a goose bump moment. And it is equally true for a young man told by an angel that his wife is pregnant by the Holy Spirit, and she will bring the Son of the Almighty God into this world.

I am daily tempted to try and do things myself, forgetting God is sovereign and in control. May

I daily be inspired by the two young, scared, but totally trusting and faithful parents of the Christ child to follow their example and simply ... trust.

***

"But Jesus immediately said to them, Take courage! It is I. Do not be afraid."

"Lord, if it is you," Peter replied, "tell me to come to you on the water."

"Come," he said.

Then Peter got down out of the boat, walked on the water and came towards Jesus. But when he saw the wind, he became afraid and beginning to sink cried, "Lord, save me!"

Immediately Jesus reached out his hand and caught him. "You of little faith," he said, "why did you doubt?"

- Matthew 14:27–36

Again the powerful message is that when you start to sink ... just trust in the Lord and put yourself in his hands.

***

"The heavens declare the glory of God; the skies proclaim his hands. Day after day they pour

forth speech; night after night, they display knowledge. There is no speech or language where their voice is not heard. Their voice goes out into all the earth, their voices to the end of the world."

- Psalm 19:1–4

The tints of red at sunrise, the perfect blue sky without a cloud, the splattered colors of the rainbow, a sunrise, a sunset. The mountains, valleys, ocean, stars. And yes, even a beautiful green perfect fairway speaks to the glory of creation.

***

"Trust in the Lord with all of your heart and lean not on your own understanding. In all your ways acknowledge him and he will make your paths straight."

- Proverbs 3:5–6

The key word here is *all!* Trust... with *all* your heart. In *all* your ways, acknowledge. There are many aspects of life that we will never understand. And *all* we can do is trust God with *all* our being in *all* things.

There are vast amounts of things good and bad in this world that I cannot understand or explain. But I know that I love God, so I trust that He is working for my good in all of the wonderful things that have blessed me as well as the painful heartbreaks of this life that make no sense.

The list of things that can cause us worry and anxiety and keep us awake at 3:00 AM seems endless at times. But the Lord has given us all the advice we need. All we need is wrapped up in trust.

***

"Do not let your hearts be troubled. Trust in God, trust also in me. In my Father's house are many rooms; if it were not so, I would have told you. I am going there to prepare a place for you. I will come back and take you to be with me that you also may be where I am."

- John 14:1-4

What these verses say to me is that Jesus is too much of a gentleman not to keep his word, therefore I trust and believe in this awesome promise. The Reverend Billy Graham has said that God has placed the yearning for heaven in our hearts and Jesus has promised heaven to all who accept him as Lord and Savior. If Jesus has made a promise, I think we can bank on it and this should fuel us with encouragement and belief.

***

"You are my servant. I have chosen you and not rejected you. So do not fear, for I am with

you; do not be dismayed for I am your God. I will strengthen you and help you. I will uphold you with my righteous right hand. All who rage against you will surely be ashamed and disgraced; those who oppose you will be as nothing and perish."
                                                    - Isaiah 41: 9–11

How powerful is this? Little ole me? I am chosen? You are with me? You will uphold me? Lord, I am not worthy, speak but the word and my soul shall be healed.

Whether it is the workplace or the home place, the mission field or somewhere in between, the Bible is full of stories where God calls a leader. The message: those God calls he equips; and those he equips he protects and delivers. He will enable your success when you are aligned with kingdom goals, working your best, and trusting in his Holy Spirit for the rest.

***

"Therefore I tell you do not worry. Who of you by worrying can add a single hour to his life? O you of little faith. So do not worry for your heavenly Father knows what you need. But seek first his kingdom and his righteousness and all these things will be given to you as well. Therefore, do not worry about tomorrow for

tomorrow will worry about itself. Each day has enough trouble of its own."
- Matthew 6:25, 27, 30, 32–34

Life can wear us down with all of its burdens, conflicts, and outright brokenness. Add to the mix responsibilities, illnesses, finances, loved ones, and the weariness factor can seem overwhelming. But we compound it all greatly by adding unnecessary worry on top of everything. And while we learn as we go that most of what we worry about never comes to pass, we still continue to worry. Not only do we take on more pain than necessary, but we also dishonor our Creator. But He knows us and knows what we want and need better than we do. Therefore, the day would be much lighter if we heeded the words of Jesus above.

God and Golf Moment

Play It as It Lies

This is a cardinal rule of golf.

You cannot improve the lie or situation where your shot has come to rest. You must play it as it lies. This often results in frustration and a feeling that "it's just not fair." Someone can hit a great towering beautiful shot towards the green but in a one-in-a-hundred random event, the ball bounces off a buried sprinkler head (water is how greens stay green) and caroms 50 yards into the nearby woods or out of bounds. Unfair!

Life can serve up some similar circumstances (death, disease, job loss, etc.), where there is no alternative but to play it as it lies despite how unfair we may think the situation.

But if we place our trust in God, unlike golf we can get some "relief." God may not take our painful situation away, but he will walk with us, carry us, and help us through our valley of darkness.

Chapter 11

FINISHING STRONG

> *"I have fought the good fight, I have finished the race. Now there is in store for me, the crown of righteousness, which the Lord the righteous judge, will award to me on that day."*
>
> - 2 Timothy 4:7–8

B obby Jones was one of the greatest golfers who ever lived, having been one of the few people to win all four major golf tournaments. He was equally respected as a total gentleman and a real tribute to both golf and life. He was born in 1902 and died in 1971. In 1948, he was diagnosed with a rare spinal cord disease which caused crippling pain, ended his golfing, and ultimately relegated him to a wheelchair. When friends and family would try to show him sympathy even touching on pity, his response was, "I have lived a charmed life thanks to golf and I have no regrets. Life is like golf. You play it as it lies." He was referring to the cardinal rule of golf. The professional golfer plays by the strictest adherence to the voluminous and at times arcane official rules of golf. But the first rule of golf is you play the ball where it lies. It may be in the fairway, in the high rough grass, behind a rock or beside a tree. The fun golfer might kick the ball out, but the professional golfer must play it as it lies. So Bobby Jones was saying that life is similar. You can be in the beautiful grass of the fairway or in the rocks of a hazard. But unfortunately in life you must also play it as it lies.

***

My mom died in 2005 at the age of eighty. She had been ill for the previous three years with a rare offshoot of ovarian cancer. It was a blurry time for her consisting of a series of powerful chemotherapy regimens that would knock a young athlete on her butt. So for an eighty-year-old, the impact was a lot of side effects and a lot of sleeping. My dad was at her side every day. My brothers and sister who lived nearby also helped out a great deal. Living about 2 hours away and still working full-time, I made it a point to see her once every one to two weeks.

I like to think of myself as mentally strong, spiritually strong, and even physically strong for my size. But I also think of myself as emotionally weak. By that I mean I am a chicken when it comes to dealing with pain and loss of those I love and hold dear. It is very difficult to see them cry or be in pain. So this was something I was going to have to face into and handle.

To my pleasant surprise, the Lord of the Impossible stepped in when I needed him most in life and carried me through the fire. There is a verse in the Bible that reads, "I will be with you when you go through the fires." Note that it does not say *if* but rather *when.* Because besides the proverbial death and taxes, the other thing that you can be 100 percent certain of is fiery life trials. But God says in so many words to not be afraid because I will be there to carry you through. True to his word, he absolutely carried me through the last very difficult year of my mom's life and particularly the last few months.

During these last months, I would talk almost every day with Mom, Dad, or my siblings. Some days she was doing good and the next day she could be doing awful in terms of discomfort or side effects. So there was a cycle of good days and bad days. Typically, the pattern would go something like this: I would be planning to go down and see her on a Wednesday and when I checked in on Tuesday it was a bad day or a very bad day. On the Wednesday, as I left work midday with a sense of dread, I would find myself driving below the speed limit (very out of character). As I approached the house, I would stop at the local Starbucks and brace myself with a tall bold coffee and some sugary scone. I would envision the worst of what my visit might be like. Finally I would say to myself, "Come on, stop procrastinating, man up and go see your mother!" And off I would go the final two miles and pull into the driveway.

So here is one way the Lord of the Impossible showed up and carried me through the fire—I never had a bad visit. She would be sitting up in the family room, maybe nod off here or there, but lucid. By "lucid" I mean still able to give me advice on how to raise my family, what I should be doing with so and so at work, and whether or not she liked the tie I was wearing. She was a trip even towards the end.

My mom only went to church on Christmas and Easter, but she made it a point that we would go to church with my dad every Sunday. At least a couple of times as an adult I would ask her why she did not go to church and she would raise her voice a tad and say, "It is none of your darn business. Leave me alone!" Or one time she said, "Do I bother you about renouncing your faith?" And I would have to explain, "Mom, I did not renounce my faith. When I got divorced I was excommunicated from the Catholic Church, but I still loved my God so I joined a Protestant church which did not have a similar restriction." She said, "Well, I am not sure I understand any of that but fine."

But in the final months, something was bothering me. I needed to know that my mom believed in Jesus as the Son of God and Redeemer of all. I needed to know she knew and was certain of where she was going to spend her eternity. So during one of my visits, I gathered up the courage to broach the subject. In her classic and loving way, she cut me off by leaning over to her nightstand and picked up a devotional that someone had given her. She patted the book and said, "Me and Jesus are doing just fine. You don't have to worry about me." I have to tell you that I believed her and it was like this huge weight was lifted off me. It was similar to when the priest surprised me after my grandfather's funeral, telling me how much my grandfather loved Jesus. It made me reflect that perhaps these older-generation Italians were just not as open about their faith and held it as something very private between them and their Creator. Anyway, I felt very relieved. "Just don't worry about me. What else do you want to talk about?" she said.

***

It was June of 2005 when we were told by Hospice that the end was near. All my siblings and I headed back to the house we all had been raised in. My mom was in a coma the last three days, so we weren't sure at all that she even knew we were there. But we knew it was where we were supposed to be. And yet again my loving God showed up when I needed him most and in ways I could not envision. Dad and Mom, Rich, Rob, Adrienne, Bruce, Mark, and I were all back together again. Amidst the pain, there was a hidden sense of joy (not happiness) as we all realized what a blessing this was. All the wonderful memories, the joys, and a full understanding of what a rare privilege it was to be raised in the family of Bill and Anna Cordivari. As adults, we had all been witnesses to close friends who had much pain and heartache associated with dysfunctional families. We had come to treasure what a rare jewel our family was. And we siblings were full of total gratitude to our parents who had made it all possible.

On the last day, around mid-morning, the hospice nurse told us "it" was very near... "a matter of hours... if not minutes." You would think we would have been prepared by now, but it was still such a gut punch hearing it from the expert and realizing that the last veneer of denial has been stripped away.

We all gathered and I asked my dad if I could read one of my most consoling Bible readings, which is Psalm 23. He nodded silently in the affirmative. We all held hands as I read,

The Lord is my shepherd, I shall not be in want. He makes me lie down in green pastures,
He leads me beside quiet waters, he restores my soul.
He guides me in paths of righteousness for his name sake.
Even though I walk through the valley of the shadow of death,
I will fear no evil, for thou are with me;
Your rod and your staff, they comfort me.

You prepare a table before me in the presence of my enemies.
You anoint my head with oil; my cup overflows.
Surely goodness and love will follow me all the days of my life.
And I will dwell in the house of the Lord forever.

And then we each took our individual turns saying goodbye to Mom. Obviously it was a moment of overwhelming grief and sorrow, but also joy as we each could recount to her in our personal way how much she meant to us. And as the emotions swept over me and I felt myself tumbling into the abyss, the most miraculous thing occurred. At the point of my maximum grief, she squeezed my hand. I opened my eyes and looked at her, but her eyes were still closed as they had been for most of the last week. But in her dying moments, she found a last ounce of strength to squeeze my hand as if to say, *It is okay, and everything will be okay. For me and all of you.* I felt joy. I felt relief and I felt the presence of an awesome God carrying me through the inferno when I most needed him. "Lord, I am not worthy that you would save and comfort a wretch like me."

And then... my mom was gone.

***

In the months before she died, she prepared my dad. Some ways were practical, like making sure he knew how to cook certain meals, and some ways were humorous, like when she told him that he could remarry if he wanted. But then every day she would add another stipulation of what was forbidden. One day it was, "I told him he can't just marry any old floozie" (there was that word again!). Another day she said, "And I told him he cannot divert any of my children or grandchildren's money to her." Can I say, with all love and affection, my mom was a pisser!

(You laugh so hard you wet your pants — if I need to clarify.)

My grandmother, Jennie Cordivari, died when she was sixty-five. My grandfather, William Anthony, lived to the age of ninety-two. He was a widower for over twenty-five years and you just knew he was not going to remarry. My dad is now ninety-two and has been a widower for over a decade. It does not appear the older generation Italian men remarry. They just throw themselves completely into their families. I saw that with my grandfather and have witnessed it also with my father.

***

After my mother died, my father put up this giant collage of photos capturing the fifty-plus years that he and she were married. It was really neat, as I had rarely seen many of these photos. My mother was stunningly beautiful in her wedding photos. And there was this one particular photo that captivated me because she looked so young and vibrant with a joyful smile. I guess it stayed with me.

One night a few months after she died, I had a brief dream that I was sitting with her in heaven. It was very peaceful and she was so beautiful. I reflected that in that dream she looked like the photo I described. I went back to that photo in the collage and looked at the date on the back. She was thirty-three years old. Hmmm ... Jesus was thirty-three when he died. I would sometimes muse about what age our loved ones look in heaven. And I would say to myself, probably thirty-three. Most people still look pretty good in this world at thirty-three, so maybe thirty-three. And that was the age of my mom in my dream, me sitting with her in heaven. I am not declaring any theological teaching here, just an instinct from love and emotion. So be it, Anna Assunta Liberi Cordivari. What an awesome lady and mother. She gave us so much, including how to face the final days with strength, peace, dignity and joy. Gone from this earth but not a day goes by that she is forgotten. And we live as believers with the assurance that we will be reunited in heaven. Jesus said so and that is good enough for me.

"Do not let your hearts be troubled. Trust in God, trust also in me. In my Father's house there are many rooms; if it were not so I would have told you. I am going there to prepare a place for you. And if I go and prepare a place for you, I will come back and take you to be with me that you may also be where I am."

- John 14:1-3

Epilogue

HEADING HOME: WALKING DOWN THE EIGHTEENTH FAIRWAY

A professional golf tournament is a grueling affair. Generally, the format is four eighteen-hole matches played on Thursday through Sunday. It is extremely difficult to keep your golf swing, tempo, and mental edge performing at its highest level through the course of a tournament. Most of the participants will experience disappointment, setbacks, and even despair when victory may have seemed so close only to disappear with one errant shot, mental miscue, or bad bounce. But there will be a winner. On any given Sunday, someone will have prevailed against all of these challenges. And the gallery of spectators who have been following their favorites around the course all of these days now have nowhere else to be but lining the eighteenth and final fairway as the leader or co-leaders appear over a hill and start their ascent to the final green. The crowd cheers loudly in appreciation of the rare skills the participants have displayed to arrive at this point in the match. For any golfers in the stands, whether casual or serious, there is a shared knowledge and appreciation of what it took to get here: the persistence, perseverance, stamina, and unwavering commitment to professional golf at its highest level.

The crowd includes the fans, family and children of the players, golf association officials, TV cameras and personalities, and other various sponsors and golf dignitaries. All are witnesses to the final act of excellence about to take place as one of the players will sink the final winning putt for victory. For many professional golfers as well as "the band of believers...and golfers" I know, this moment captures the essence of faith, family, and fairways.

> "Therefore since we are surrounded by such a great cloud of witnesses, let us throw off everything that hinders and the sin that so easily entangles and let us run with perseverance the race marked out for us. Let us fix our eyes on Jesus, the author and perfecter of our faith, who for the joy set before him endured the cross, scorning its shame and sat down at the right hand of the throne of God. Consider him who endured such opposition from sinful men, so that you will not grow weary and lose heart."

I love this verse from the book of Hebrews. And I remember a milestone event in my life that first captured it for me.

***

My wife threw me a surprise party on my fiftieth birthday. I still remember the entrance vividly all these years later. I was completely caught off guard as I entered the side room of a favorite restaurant. The lights came on and the crowd screamed "Surprise!" And oh, was I! I almost passed out from sensory overload. As my mind processed what was happening in the first milliseconds, my eyes took in all the people I saw—people who I cared for and loved from every aspect of my life. My mom and dad were there, as well as all my brothers and sister; all my children, some having travelled great distances to be there. But also my best friends from work, church, neighborhood, and golf. All their smiling and cheering faces. What an unforgettable night and moment.

I remember thinking, *Maybe this is what it is like entering heaven.* Surprise? Well, I hope not the surprise part! But being surrounded by such a great cloud of witnesses who have been faithful servants enjoying the master's reward and now getting to reunite with them. Some we may have forgotten temporarily as the years on earth have gone by, and some we may even be surprised by. But it will be awesome beyond earthly comprehension.

"Well done good and faithful servant. You have been faithful with a few things; I will put you in charge of many things. Come and share in your master's happiness."

***

This would be a good place to finish the story started in Chapter 1…

Dad, Rich, Rob and I are driving back to the Philadelphia area after our daylong golf outing in Maryland. It was a hot night with the cool air conditioning blowing on our faces, and nearly everyone falling asleep except our driver. We had all settled into our rhythm and there was an air of peaceful silence. Then we hear this small voice come from the backseat, my father inquiring, "One more time. Guys, why wouldn't you play from the green tees?" As the eldest son speaking for the trio, I responded: "Dad, here is the deal: we are just not ready to admit we are old yet." (We were not yet ready to admit we were old and ready to accept all of the anxious associations that come with it.)

But as believers and people of faith, we should have no fear of getting old and no fear of what is beyond. Jesus has conquered the grave and there is an eternal reward for all who accept him as their Lord and Savior. My favorite verse about eternity comes from our brother in Christ, the apostle Paul in 1 Corinthians 15:55

"Oh death where is thy victory? Oh grave, where is thy sting?"

And with the full knowledge of this assurance, the verses that can fuel our joy and gratitude each day on this earth also come from Paul in Philippians 4:

"Rejoice in the Lord always, I will say it again: Rejoice! Let your gentleness be evident to all. The Lord is near. Do not be anxious about anything but in everything by prayer and petition, with thanksgiving, present your requests to God. And the peace of God which transcends all understanding will guard your hearts and your minds in Christ Jesus."

What more can I add? Nothing but Amen!